MODERN NATIONS OF THE WORLD

BELIZE

BY DEBRA A. MILLER

LUCENT BOOKS

An imprint of Thomson Gale, a part of The Thomson Corporation

THOMSON GALE™

Detroit • New York • San Francisco • San Diego • New Haven, Conn. • Waterville, Maine • London • Munich

On cover: Colorful buildings line a narrow street in Belize's capital, Belize City.

For more information, contact
Lucent Books
27500 Drake Rd.
Farmington Hills, MI 48331-3535
Or you can visit our Internet site at http://www.gale.com

LIBRARY OF CONGRESS CATALOGING-IN-PUBLICATION DATA

Miller, Debra A.
Belize / by Debra A. Miller.
p. cm. — (Modern nations of the world)
Includes bibliographical references and index.
ISBN 1-59018-726-1 (hardcover : alk. paper)
1. Belize—Juvenile literature. I. Title. II. Series.
F1443.2.M55 2005
972.82—dc22

2004022543

Printed in the United States of America

Contents

Introduction

An Untouched Jewel

Belize, a tiny country in Central America, is a paradise, one of the last places in the world where nature has not been significantly altered by human habitation. Some of the most well known of the country's natural riches are its lush rain forests, its 175 idyllic islands, and its barrier reef—the second largest barrier reef in the world. Belize also has miles of navigable rivers, countless marshes and wetland areas, flat agricultural plains, sandy white beaches, and soaring mountains that are marked by numerous caves and spectacular waterfalls. Moreover, jaguars and other endangered species still prowl the country's extensive jungles. Belize's tropical forests are also home to more than 500 varieties of birds as well as over 250 types of wild orchids and an untold number of other plants, animals, insects, and fungi. In Belize's rivers, wetlands, and coastal waters, and around its spectacular coral reefs and islands, swim many varieties of exotic fish, shellfish, and other marine creatures. In all these habitats, there is very little pollution. In fact, Belize is one of the least polluted places on Earth.

Most of Belize's land is undeveloped, and Belize has been able to maintain its natural beauty largely because of its small population. As journalist Meb Cutlack describes,

> Scenically the country is a wonderland, an untouched wilderness which the overzealous twentieth century has left alone. . . . It is [the lack] of population which has kept Belize almost unspoilt to this day, allowing hundreds of square miles of forest, savannah, wetlands and [islands] to remain intact, free from pesticides and pollutants, so that many secrets remain hidden, even in her soil, and in the plant and animal life which thrives in the rare privacy of nature.[1]

Belize's underdevelopment is a result of its unique history. The area was claimed originally by Spain, but was never really settled by that country. Spain eventually permitted British settlers to extract timber from the region but otherwise restricted Britain from developing or establishing agriculture there. Belize eventually became a British colony, but even then it continued to be exploited mostly for its forest resources. Timber was accessible and easy to float down Belize's many rivers; meanwhile, the nation's often isolated flatlands (which are ripe for farming) were mostly neglected. Indeed, agriculture became important to Belize only in the 1960s, after timber was largely depleted, and the country had to turn to growing sugarcane as a revenue replacement. Because of the focus on forest resources and later sugarcane, other activities that could have harmed the environment, such as big industry, have never really been established in the country. As a result, by the time Belize became an independent nation in 1981, it had largely missed much of the aggressive industrial development (and accompanying habitat

Thatch huts and palm trees dot the pristine coastline along Glovers Reef in Belize. Belize is one of the world's least developed countries.

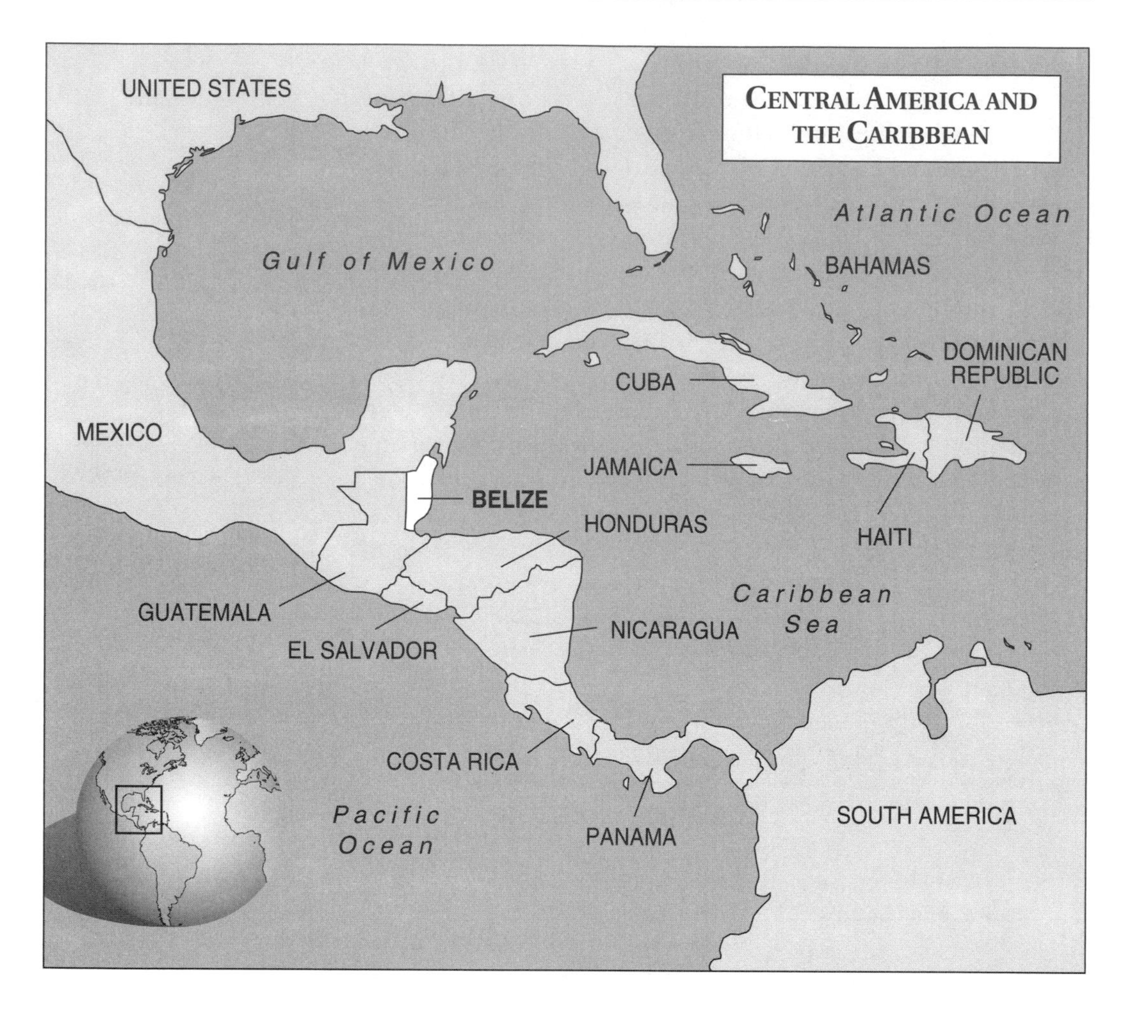

destruction and pollution) that marked the twentieth century for many other countries.

Although the country's underdevelopment preserved much of Belize's natural environment, it also has had some negative effects. Poverty, unemployment, and inadequate education and health care are serious problems for the tiny nation because Belize has limited financial resources to take care of its people's needs. The lack of income also makes the country dependent on foreign aid and investment, which sometimes is accompanied by unwanted foreign influences on its culture and economy.

The people of Belize realize, however, that the country's pristine environment is mostly a blessing. Belizeans are very concerned about protecting their environment through legislation and regulation. Capitalizing on its natural riches, Belize is becoming a leader in ecotourism, a type of tourism that attracts visitors interested in experiencing the wild, untouched environment. Promoting ecotourism, therefore, means that Belize is avoiding large-scale building and development and is very concerned with preserving the ecology for future generations to enjoy. Today, many parts of Belize lack the luxuries, such as good roads, five-star hotels, and fine restaurants, that are found in more developed countries. Yet for those who value nature, Belize beckons. Tourists flock to the country to see its many natural wonders. Divers, in particular, are attracted by Belize's virtually unmatched coral reefs and islands. Scientists travel deep into Belize's rain forests hoping to discover new types of plant and animal life. Wildlife experts come to study endangered species, and botanists are amazed by the endless number of herbal medicines produced by the jungles. In addition, photographers are drawn by the country's unique and beautiful sights. For many, then, Belize is truly one of the last remaining jewels in the natural world.

1 A Diverse Land

Belize is a relatively new nation located on the Caribbean coast of northern Central America. Lying just south of the Yucatán Peninsula, Belize is bordered by the Caribbean Sea to the east, Mexico to the north, and Guatemala to the west and south. The country is tiny, only about 174 miles long and 68 miles wide, or roughly the size of the state of New Hampshire. Its population numbers only 272,945, which is about the size of a small American city. Although small in both size and population, Belize nevertheless is a land of great beauty and diversity.

Northern Belize

Northern Belize, the country's most developed region and the area where most of its people live, is a flat plain extending from the coast to the country's northern and western borders. Several of the country's towns and cities are found along this northern coastline, including Belize City, once the country's capital and still its busiest and most populous city. Although the land in this area rarely rises more than two hundred feet above sea level, it does include occasional small hills and rolling terrain. Eighteen rivers and many smaller streams drain through these lowlands. As a result, the northern coastline is broken by numerous humid and insect-infested swamps and lagoons that form where rivers and streams empty into the sea. Many of these swampy areas are filled with mangroves, a tropical tree whose roots grow underwater.

Farther inland, the land is marked by a limestone plateau. In this area, the soil quality is sometimes poor, but in many places fertile soils are deposited by the many rivers and streams. Because of the flat landscape, pockets of good soil, and abundant rainfall, this area is Belize's agricultural heartland and the center of its sugarcane industry. Citrus fruits and bananas are also grown here, and where the right soil is available, some rice, beans, and vegetables. In addition, a few dairy cattle, beef cattle, and poultry farms have been established.

Cultivated land, however, takes up only a small part of northern Belize. As much as 90 percent of the land here is still covered by forests. Most of this area was once covered by mixed hardwood trees such as logwood and mahogany. Today, many of the most commercially marketable tree species have now been harvested, and large parts of northern Belize are covered with scrub pine. Nevertheless, the western side of the northern flatlands is still covered with large, pristine

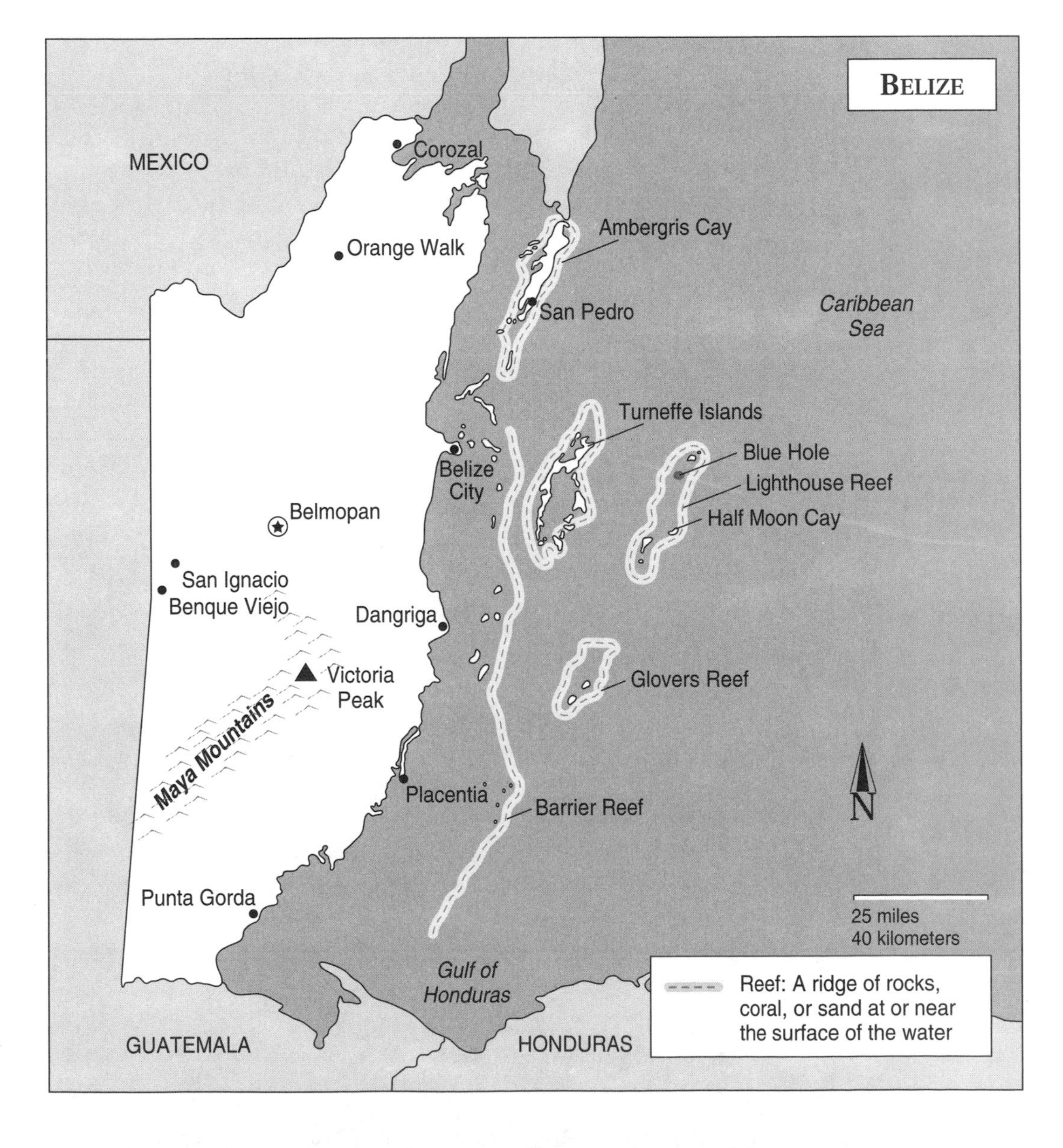

tropical rain forest reserves. Here, huge trees form a shady canopy that is home to hundreds of unique plants, mammals, birds, and reptiles. Monkeys swing from the trees and eat bananas and other tropical fruit, jaguars roam the jungle floor, and bright-colored birds can be seen and heard everywhere.

THE MAYA MOUNTAINS

To the south, the land in Belize rises to form the Maya Mountains. This large limestone mountain range runs north to south and dominates the southern part of the country. The highest points are Victoria Peak (3,680 feet) and Doyle's Delight (3,851 feet). Both of these peaks are located in the Cockscomb Range, a group of granite and quartz peaks in the northeastern part of the mountain area. Largely unpopulated and not even completely explored, the Maya Mountains are covered with rain forests and contain many fast-running rivers and streams.

In addition to the rich treasures of plant and animal life in these upland forests, the area has become known for its magnificent waterfalls, some of which fall more than one

A tour guide points out stalactite formations in a cave in the Maya Mountains, which dominate the landscape of southern Belize.

thousand feet. The mountain areas are also known for their hundreds of caves, caverns, and sinkholes. These underground openings were formed in places where the streams disappear underground; over time, the flowing waters hollowed out the soft limestone. Some of the caves are quite large. A cave located in the northwest part of the mountain range called Rio Frio, for example, has one chamber that arches to 65 feet tall and measures 525 feet long.

Between the mountains and the sea is a low-lying coastal plain about fifteen miles wide. Several towns are located here, including Dangriga, the largest southern town; Placentia, a banana-exporting port; and Punta Gorda, the country's southernmost urban area. Belize's current capital city, Belmopan, however, is situated inland just north of the Maya mountain range along the banks of the Belize River.

THE BELIZE COAST

The coast of Belize is another wonder of nature. In the shallow waters just off the coast is a string of small but beautiful islands called the cays (pronounced "kees"). These islands are mostly made of sand, and they help protect the mainland from storms coming in from the sea. Some are submerged and covered with mangrove trees, while others rise above the water and contain vegetation such as coconut palms. Most of the cays are uninhabited, but a few are home to tourist resorts. For example, the small tourist town of San Pedro is located on one of the larger, palm-covered cays called Ambergris Cay.

The cays are located on top of a vast, 150-mile-long barrier reef that is second in size only to Australia's Great Barrier Reef. The underwater reef is made from coral—a hard, crusty collection of calcium-rich skeletons formed by colonies of small living organisms called polyps. As a colony grows, it pushes up and out, expanding the size of the coral formation about a half-inch per year. As marine biologist Ellen McRae explains,

> [The] structural framework [of the barrier reef] is composed of limestone, on which billions of individual coral polyps form colonies connected by living tissue. Each polyp consists of a set of tentacles, a mouth, and a gut perched atop a limestone skeleton. The polyps have cells on the outside of their bodies that secrete calcium carbonate. As the colony grows, the polyps build

> their skeletons from underneath, pushing themselves up or out into a myriad of sizes and shapes.[2]

About ten miles off the barrier reef, several ring-shaped coral formations, called atolls, rise out of the ocean waters. The largest of these, the Turneffe Islands, lies about forty-five miles east of Belize City. The Turneffe Islands atoll is thirty-five miles long and features numerous reefs, cays, and a protected, central lagoon. About twelve miles farther out to sea are two other spectacular and pristine atolls: Lighthouse Reef and Glovers Reef. Lighthouse Reef is known for its lagoon, which contains an enormous underwater hole. Called the Blue Hole, this formation has a diameter of about 1,000 feet and a depth of 400 feet. Partway down, the hole opens into a remarkable underwater cavern featuring numerous gigantic stalactites, which are mineral deposits that look like icicles hanging from the cavern's roof.

All the barrier reef areas are teeming with exotic marine plant and animal life. These sites are admired by divers and snorklers for their intense color and great beauty. They are known around the world as one of the best diving and ecotourist destinations. Altogether, the cays and atolls form approximately 212 square miles of territory, making up about 2.4 percent of Belize's total landmass of 8,867 square miles.

Rivers, Streams, and Wetlands

Another of Belize's natural riches is its river system, which includes several major rivers, countless streams, and numerous lagoons and wetlands. The northernmost part of Belize is drained by two major rivers: the Hondo, which marks the border with Mexico, and the New River, a navigable river that widens into a large lagoon near the Guatemalan border. Farther south, just north of the Maya Mountains, runs the Belize River, which is the country's largest. It enters the sea just five miles north of Belize City. In the south, heavy rainfall and steep mountains produce a number of shorter, faster-running, and less-navigable rivers, including the Monkey, Deep, Grande, Moho, and Sarstoon rivers. Of these, the Sarstoon River is the longest, forming Belize's southern border.

Since ancient times, Belize's rivers and tributaries have been important for trade. The ancient Maya settled near the

MARINE LIFE IN BELIZE

Living in Belize's extensive coral reefs are numerous underwater plants and grasses that provide a home to a fantastic array of unique marine life. In this environment are lobsters and crabs, other shellfish such as barnacles and conch, and many dazzling fish species in every possible size, shape, and color. Two of the most common types of fish found here are the grouper, a three-foot-long brown fish with lighter brown vertical stripes, and seventy-four varieties of angelfish, a brightly colored smaller fish with delicate fins that look like angel wings. Whale sharks can also be found during certain seasons. They are the largest known fish species and can grow to be more than fifty feet long and weigh more than twenty tons. The reef waters in Belize are also home to two mammal species. One is the dolphin, a playful and intelligent animal that often delights tourists with its antics. The manatee, or sea cow, is another tourist favorite. A distant cousin to the elephant, the manatee is gentle but big, sometimes growing as large as seven feet long and four hundred pounds. The manatee was once hunted for food but is now protected by environmental laws.

A diver explores a coral reef along an underwater ridge off the Belizean coast.

rivers, and later traders used the rivers to transport goods from the interior to the coast. Both the New River and the Belize River, for example, were used by early European settlers to transport timber goods to market. The Belize River, in fact, is probably the country's most important river because it is navigable all the way to the Guatemalan border, making it the main channel of commerce and communication between the country's interior and the coast.

Belize's river system also played a vital role in cultivation and civilization. Many of the rivers deposited fertile soil on their banks, providing the basis for agriculture and human settlement. The Sibun River, which drains the northeastern edge of the Maya Mountains, and the New River, which runs through Belize's sugar-growing areas, created very fertile regions. Indeed, most of Belize's interior towns and cities are located in the north near rivers because rivers provided the conditions crucial to both settlement and shipping.

Belize's wetlands, which include freshwater marshes in the northern part of the country as well as saline lagoons and swamps along the coast, are also important. They provide a natural type of flood control by allowing floodwaters to spread out over a wide area. They also function as soil collectors, preventing river sediments from moving out to sea.

THE BLUE HOLE

One of the most striking sites for divers in Belize is located about sixty miles off the coast from Belize City, in the center of Lighthouse Reef. Called the Blue Hole, it is an almost circular hole in the ocean floor measuring more than 1,000 feet across and 400 feet deep. The Blue Hole is part of what was once an above-water, dry cave system during the Ice Age, when huge glaciers covered large parts of the earth. The cave was flooded when the great glaciers melted, creating a fascinating and beautiful site. A dive into the Blue Hole reveals enormous stalagmites and stalactites similar to those that might be found in mountain caves. Among these cave formations live a variety of sea creatures, including sponges, barracuda, corals, angelfish, and sharks, which often patrol the hole's edge.

The Blue Hole, an underwater cave located on Lighthouse Reef, is extremely popular with divers.

The rain forests of Belize are home to many diverse species of endangered animals, including the jaguar.

In addition, wetlands provide a habitat for a myriad of unique plant, marine, and animal life, including over 540 species of both migratory and resident bird species that depend on these waters for their survival. Many types of birds, from hummingbirds to ospreys and ducks, come to Belize's wetlands after flying thousands of miles from Northern Hemisphere locations such as Canada and the northern United States. For some bird species, Belize is a nesting spot. For other species, the country is a stopover and resting place where birds can feed on fish, insects, and other types of food to allow them to continue traveling even farther south.

FORESTS, PLANTS, AND ANIMALS

Belize's vast rain forest ecosystem is located in both the western part of northern Belize and the southern mountains. This ecosystem may be the country's most important natural resource. One of the most remarkable rain forests in the world, it supports a bounty of plant and animal life, including many threatened and endangered species. The Macal River valley in western Belize, for example, is one of the most pristine and fragile habitats in all of Central America. More than a dozen rare and endangered animal and bird species can be found here.

The rain forest system also plays a significant role in cleaning the air and moderating the world's weather systems. The forest plants do this by absorbing carbon dioxide created by the burning of fossil fuels and then emitting fresh oxygen. As travel writer Ben Greensfelder notes, "Tropical forests have been called the 'lungs of the planet'—by converting carbon dioxide into oxygen, they purify and enrich the air we breathe."[3] In addition, the rain forest offers scientists vital research opportunities, from new sources of healing drugs to information about global warming.

The forest ecosystem is made up of tropical broadleaf trees such as mahogany, cedar, nargusta, poisonwood, cotton tree, mylady, sapodilla, Santa Maria, and many others.

THE THREAT TO BELIZE'S RAIN FORESTS

Belize's rain forests are one of the world's most magnificent and complex ecosystems, providing habitats for an extraordinary assortment of animal life, trees, plants, and insects. Throughout the country's history, however, the forests have been threatened by human activities. During the Mayan civilization, for example, many of the forests were cleared to make room for agriculture. The disappearance of that civilization allowed the forests to regenerate. Next, the rain forests were exploited by the Europeans, particularly the British, first for logwood (used to create a dye for wool textiles in Britain) and later for mahogany. Early on, the timber was felled by hand and floated down the rivers; the development of machines, however, led to rapid cutting that soon depleted the forests. The mahogany industry declined by the mid–twentieth century, allowing trees to grow back. Today, however, Belize is once again allowing commercial cutting of its forests. In 1995 a twenty-year logging license was awarded to Atlantic Industries, a Malaysian company. Although the contract places limits on the age and spacing of trees that can be cut, the decision has been criticized by environmental groups, who doubt the government's ability to adequately police the logging activities.

Although they are rooted in shallow surface soils, some of these trees grow to over 150 feet tall. The tall trees form a dense, multilayered canopy that filters the sunlight and provides a moist, humid environment for smaller plants such as ferns, climbing vines, and shrubs that grow on the jungle floor. Other plants that grow in this environment include hundreds of varieties of beautiful and often highly perfumed orchids as well as bromeliads, which are vibrantly colored hanging plants whose leaves take nutrients and moisture from the air. When dead leaves, bark, and other debris from the plant life fall to the ground, they provide a home for a multitude of ants, beetles, termites, spiders, and other insects. Also, these materials soon decompose and create a fertile place for tree and plant seeds to grow.

Countless animals are found in the rain forest, including a number of endangered species, such as the jaguar, the howler monkey, and the tapir. Jaguars are large, black-spotted cats that can grow to be six feet long and weigh up to 250 pounds. They are the main predators in the jungle and they feed on smaller animals—everything from mice and birds to much larger creatures. Another endangered species, the black howler monkey, is known locally as a baboon. The black howler is a large monkey that lives low in the forest canopy with family groups of four to eight members. The animal gets its name from the sounds it makes to defend its territory—a fierce howling or growling that is one of the loudest and most frightening animal sounds in the Belize forests. The tapir, or mountain cow, is a stout animal that stands about four feet high, weighs as much as 600 pounds, and uses a trunklike snout to grab leaves for food. Other animals in the rain forest include the highly poisonous fer-de-lance snake, bats, turtles, rats, anteaters, armadillos, and many species of birds.

The rain forest also is home to many ruins of the Mayan culture, an ancient people who built a great civilization in the area about A.D. 250. The remains of one of the ancient Maya's most important cities, Caracol, is found here, along with many other major ruins, such as Cahal Pech, Xunantunich, El Pilar, and Chechem-Ha. In addition, one of the largest and most spectacular of all excavated Mayan sites, Tikal, is located only about fifty miles (eighty kilometers) from Belize's western border with Guatemala.

WEATHER AND CLIMATE

Belize's rich rain forest exists because of a subtropical climate that is marked by warm temperatures, high humidity, and plentiful rainfall. The temperatures in the coastal areas average about 79 degrees Fahrenheit and are eased by cooling ocean breezes. Nevertheless, temperatures here can reach as high as about 90 degrees Fahrenheit in the summer shade to as low as 55 degrees during November through February. Temperatures can be much higher inland, often exceeding 100 degrees. On the other hand, higher elevations, such as parts of the Maya Mountains, stay relatively cool year-round. Especially in the summers, high humidity in Belize, typically as high as 85 to 90 percent, often makes the heat feel quite oppressive. This is especially true in what is called the *mauger* season, a short period in August when the winds die down, temperatures rise, and mosquitoes come out in swarms.

Although weather patterns can vary, the country has two well-defined seasons—the wet season and the dry season—that are marked by changes in humidity and rainfall. The dry (or winter) season, when rainfall is light, usually lasts from November to April or May. The wet (or summer) season,

This photo of the aftermath of the 1931 hurricane that struck Belize City shows a pile of rubble that includes oil drums, boats, and the remains of houses.

which typically lasts from June to October, brings considerably more rain. During this time, southern Belize usually experiences significantly more rain than the north. For example, the north gets only about 5 inches of rainfall each year, while rainfall in the south averages about 180 inches per year. Rainfall can also vary from year to year. Towns in southern Belize might get 300 inches of rain one year and only 100 inches the next year.

Belize's subtropical location makes it vulnerable to ferocious storms and hurricanes during the wet season. Sometimes these storms destroy entire cities. In 1931, for example, a major hurricane hit Belize City, the country's then-capital and most important city. The storm destroyed at least two-thirds of all buildings in the city and killed more than one thousand people. In 1955 Hurricane Janet leveled Corozal, another coastal city. Just six years later, Hurricane Hattie struck the Belize coast, carrying winds of 150 miles per hour and pushing a wall of seawater 14 feet high. This hurricane destroyed Belize City for a second time, prompting Belize to relocate its capital inland to Belmopan. The most recent destructive hurricane to hit Belize was Hurricane Greta, which in 1978 caused extensive damage along the southern coast.

CITIES IN BELIZE

Although a large number of Belizeans live in rural areas, much of Belize's population lives in just eight urban areas. More than 30 percent live in Belize City. A port located on the country's swampy northern coast, Belize City is the economic hub of Belize. It was founded in the early 1700s by English settlers at the mouth of the Belize River and was the main port for the early logwood and mahogany trade. Until it was hit by hurricanes in the early twentieth century, it was also the country's capital. Today, it remains Belize's commercial and cultural center. Much of the country's imports and exports come through this port, and its cultural attractions include a quaint colonial quarter with historic and government buildings, a riverside art gallery, a zoo containing more than sixty indigenous Belizean animals in a lush natural setting, and several museums showcasing the country's link with the sea. Most people who live in Belize City speak English.

The seven other largest cities, in order of decreasing size, are Orange Walk, Corozal, Dangriga, Belmopan, San Ignacio,

This photograph gives a bird's-eye view of San Pedro, a city on Ambergris Cay, one of Belize's many islands.

Benque Viejo, and Punta Gorda. Orange Walk, a northern town located inland on the New River about fifty-seven miles north of Belize City, is the country's second largest commercial center. Its economy is based on Belize's sugarcane industry, and at harvest time a stream of trucks can be seen rumbling to and from its sugar refinery. It was settled in the 1860s by emigrants from Mexico and remains predominantly Spanish speaking.

Even farther to the north, about ninety miles from Belize City and close to the Mexican border, is Corozal, a quiet coastal community. Like Orange Walk, it was founded in the mid-1800s by Spanish-speaking refugees from Mexico's Yucatán Peninsula. It is a developing tourist center for Belize's ecotourism industry.

About forty-five miles southwest of Belize City is Belmopan, Belize's capital. It was established as the country's inland capital following the devastation of Belize City by Hurricane Hattie in 1961, and today it is a growing center for business and commerce.

Dangriga, San Ignacio, Banque Viejo, and Punta Gorda are all southern towns. San Ignacio and Benque Viejo are located deep in the interior of Belize, near the Guatemalan border. San Ignacio is a lively resort town with shops, restaurants, and tourist attractions such as caving, hiking, and horseback riding. Benque Viejo is a quiet artistic community and home to the country's main book publishers and music producers. Dangriga and Punta Gorda are both small coastal communities with beautiful ocean views.

Belize's cities and towns are culturally varied, and although sometimes a bit rundown or rustic looking, they often feature towering palm trees, lush foliage, and colorful, quaint buildings. They clearly contribute to what most observers consider Belize's most striking characteristic—its great diversity and natural beauty.

2

Belize's Colonial Past

The area today called Belize was first settled thousands of years ago by the ancient Maya, who cleared large parts of the jungle forests and developed an impressive agricultural civilization throughout Central America. Centuries later, Belize's rich forest resources attracted new explorers from Europe who established logging camps to exploit the area's valuable timber. The area evolved into a British settlement, and later a British colony. These developments greatly affected Belize's political, social, and economic future.

The Ancient Maya

The earliest inhabitants of Belize were the Maya, a people descended from nomads who migrated to the Americas from Asia thirty-five thousand years ago. These nomads reached the North American continent by crossing over the Bering Strait, on a frozen land bridge that once linked Asia and North America. They wandered south, adapting over many centuries from a nomadic culture to village farmers, and creating many different cultures throughout Central America. As scholar Lynn V. Foster explains, "Mayan civilization [was] the single most important culture of ancient Central America. Mayan city-states ruled northern Central America in what is now Belize, Guatemala, western Honduras, and much of El Salvador while countless small chiefdoms fragmented the southern part of the [area] into a kaleidoscope of cultures."[4]

The Mayan civilization reached its peak between A.D. 250 and 1000; it numbered at one point as many as two to three million people. Even the small Belize area was home to at least 400,000 people. The Maya were accomplished farmers, traders, astronomers, builders, writers, and artisans. They cleared the rain forests, developed systems of irrigation, and raised a variety of crops, such as sweet potatoes, beans, and maize (corn). They traded various goods and ideas with their neighbors in southern Central America. In addition, the Maya were advanced mathematicians and astronomers who, without the aid of telescopes, were able to predict eclipses, solstices, and other celestial events with great accuracy. They put this knowledge to use to create a type of farmer's almanac, which was used to predict the best times for planting and harvesting. This almanac was not the Maya's only written record. Today's archaeologists know about Mayan culture partly because the Maya recorded much of their history in writing, using an advanced system of hieroglyphics that they invented.

The Maya are perhaps best known, however, for their art and architecture. They built magnificent, carefully planned

This ancient illustration depicts Mayan warriors capturing enemies. Chronic warfare likely contributed to the collapse of Mayan civilization.

stone cities in the jungle landscape. These cities contained expansive public plazas, soaring temples to the gods, and comfortable living compounds. Their architecture was refined and graceful. Arches gave height to interior spaces, and buildings were capped by mansard roofs, a steep type of roof that the Maya invented. Most often, buildings were constructed of limestone, which was covered with plaster and then painted. Inside, artistic murals and stone relief sculptures depicting people, animals, gods, and highly developed geometric patterns often decorated the walls. The cities also typically had canals and reservoirs that provided residents with fresh water for bathing and irrigation. Many of these astounding Mayan cities are still standing in Belize and neighboring countries. They have been eroded by time and the elements, however, and today many are covered by vines and trees. A few have been excavated and are popular sites for tourists.

For unknown reasons, the Mayan culture declined in the tenth century. Slowly, populations decreased, cities were abandoned, public building activities stopped, and social and economic activities withered. Archaeologists speculate that several factors may have caused the collapse, including war, natural catastrophes (such as drought), and overpopulation. Most believe that the Maya's deforestation of the rain forest combined with their growing population may have stressed the environment beyond its limit, resulting in soil erosion, malnutrition, and death. There is also evidence of frequent warfare between Mayan cities. Despite the demise of the Mayan civilization, however, some Maya survived and continued to live in a few of the Mayan settlements. Today, their descendants still form part of Belize's population.

EUROPEAN CONQUEST IN THE NEW WORLD

Centuries after the end of the great Mayan civilizations, in the sixteenth century, European explorers arrived in the Belize region of Central America. Europeans were attracted to the Americas, called the New World, because of the unspoiled natural resources they found there. The Europeans hoped to settle the wilderness and cut timber to send back to their mother countries.

The first European explorer to the region was Christopher Columbus, an Italian exploring for Spain who had first encountered the Americas in 1492 while looking for a sea route to Asia. On his fourth trip to the New World in 1502, Columbus traveled south to the Bay of Honduras and claimed the surrounding area for Spain. Just a few years later, two other Spanish explorers, Vicente Yáñez Pinzón and Juan Díaz de Solís, sailed along the Caribbean coast of Belize into the Yucatán. This initial exploration was followed by numerous other Spanish expeditions to Central America. Soon Spain had conquered and established colonies throughout the Yucatán region, including areas that are now part of Mexico, Guatemala, and Honduras.

In the Belize area, Spanish missionaries sailed up the New River to the Mayan settlement of Tipu, expecting to convert and subdue the people living there. Spanish priests built

MAYAN RUINS IN BELIZE

The Maya were prolific builders. They erected over eighty square miles of cities throughout Central America. These cities were filled with huge stone temples and elegant palaces decorated with low-relief sculptures, masks, and multicolored murals. Often, the walls of Mayan buildings also included hieroglyphic writings describing important events in the lives of their rulers. The remains of several of these ancient cities still exist in Belize. Because the small country lacks the resources to fund major archaeological digs, however, most of its Mayan ruins still lie deep under the jungle brush, waiting for excavation.

Two important, partially excavated sites are the Mayan cities of Caracol and Cahal Pech. Caracol, now recognized as one of the great Mayan cities, extends over seventy miles in southwestern Belize. Cahal Pech, north of Caracol in the town of San Ignacio, is smaller (only three acres), but it is well preserved and is believed to have been a very important Mayan trading center located in the heart of the Belize River valley. Both sites are popular tourist destinations.

The ruins of Atlan Ha stand as testimony to the great architectural skills of the Maya.

Christopher Columbus claims the island of San Salvador in the Bahamas for Spain in 1492. The Maya in Belize fiercely resisted the Spanish invasion.

churches and tried to introduce the people to Catholicism, often by force. The Maya, however, fiercely resisted the Spanish invasion, and Spain was unable to maintain effective control in Belize as it did in other parts of Central America. The Spanish were still powerful, however, and many Maya were killed, forcibly relocated, or captured and sold as slaves. In addition, large numbers of Maya were infected with deadly diseases such as smallpox and yellow fever, which had been brought by the Spaniards. The Mayan population in Belize, estimated at about 200,000 at the time of the first contact with Spain, was almost devastated by the contact with the Spanish conquerors.

SPANISH AND BRITISH RIVALRY

Other European powers such as Holland, France, and Great Britain soon began to challenge Spain's monopoly on trade and colonization in Central America. By the seventeenth century, Britain had emerged as Spain's primary threat in the western Caribbean. In 1655 Britain captured the neighboring territory of Jamaica and began sending its pirates, called buccaneers, to establish settlements along the Caribbean coast. From these settlements, the buccaneers attacked and plundered Spanish ships carrying logwood cut from the area's forests. The logwood produced a dye that was sought after in Europe for dying wool. Soon, the British began cutting and shipping their own logwood, and this became the main British industry in the Belize area for the next century. The shift from piracy to logwood harvesting was encouraged by a 1670 treaty called the Treaty of Madrid, in which Britain and other European powers agreed to suppress their piracy activities.

Thereafter, British settlements on the Belize coast became more established, but the Spanish still claimed ownership of the area. Several times during a period called the Seven Years' War the Spanish attacked British settlers and forced them to leave. Yet each time Spain failed to follow up with its own settlements, the British would return to continue their logging and trade. The prolonged war ended in 1763 with a treaty between the two countries (the Treaty of Paris) that gave Britain the right to harvest logwood but retained Spanish sovereignty over the territory.

How Belize Got Its Name

Belize's name is somewhat of a mystery. It may have been derived from the Mayan word *belix*, which means "muddy water." Many say that this aptly describes the Belize River just after a rainstorm. Others claim the name comes from another Mayan word, *belekin*, which means "toward the east." Today, Belikin is the name of the country's national beer. A third explanation is that the name comes from either the French word *balise*, which means "beacon," or the Spanish words, *bella isla*, which means "beautiful island." Yet another popular theory is that the name is a corruption of "Wallace," the name of a Scottish or English buccaneer who is said to have founded the first settlement on Belize's shores in 1638. According to this legend, Wallace was first pronounced "Vallis," because there is no "W" in Spanish, and this later mutated into Balis or Belize.

Over the next couple of decades, however, Spanish control weakened and the British presence became even more pronounced. Still, Britain feared establishing a formal colony because it did not want to provoke Spain. In the absence of a British system of government, the settlers (called Baymen) themselves began to organize elections and create a system of law to keep the peace. In 1787 two thousand additional British settlers and their slaves arrived in Belize. Soon, despite British prohibition of governmental activities, a group of the most influential and wealthy Baymen created the first legislature, called the Public Meeting. They also claimed most of the land for themselves and succeeded in having the British superintendent and overseer of the settlement, Colonel Edward Marcus Despard, suspended. Relations between the British government and the settlers remained uneasy, and the small, elite group of settlers gained ever more control.

SLAVERY AND SOCIAL CONDITIONS

The main focus of the Belize settlement was the cutting of timber. To help with this endeavor, the British imported slaves. Most slaves came from African locations such as the Congo, the Bight of Benin, and Angola. When trade shifted from logwood to mahogany at the end of the eighteenth century, even more slaves were imported to handle larger timber operations. As professor C.H. Grant notes, "The [Belize] forestry industry [was] built on African slave labor."[5] Male slaves primarily became woodcutters in the timber industry; they cut and trimmed the trees and, with the help of cattle, pulled the logs into the rivers, where they would be floated downstream to market. Female and child slaves were typically employed for domestic chores, such as cooking, housecleaning, sewing, and ironing.

Slaves were often treated badly by their white masters, and many tried to revolt, commit suicide, or simply run away into the bush. According to sociology professor O. Nigel Bolland, "Slaves . . . could relatively easily escape in Belize if they were willing to leave their families. In the eighteenth century many escaped to Yucatán, and in the early nineteenth century a steady flow of runaways went to Guatemala or down the coast to Honduras. Some runaways established . . . [their own] communities within Belize."[6]

Emancipated slaves in Barbados dance in the streets after Britain abolishes slavery in its colonies, including Belize, in 1833.

The African slaves maintained African traditions and culture when they first arrived in the Belize settlement, but slowly they were assimilated into the dominant British culture. The whites from Britain, who maintained control of the settlement's economy and politics, encouraged this assimilation. Indeed, many whites fathered children by their black slaves, producing offspring who were lighter skinned than the full-blooded Africans. This process eventually created a new, mixed-race Creole society in Belize. Adding to the Creole population were a small number of free black immigrants. These free blacks were Africans who had been liberated by Spanish slavers and blacks of African descent who traveled to the Belize area from the British West Indies.

In 1833 Britain enacted a law to abolish slavery in all of its colonies, including the Belize settlement. The law provided for a five-year transition to full emancipation, which occurred in 1838. After emancipation, however, many economic and political restrictions were placed on the now legally free Creole people. For example, most were not allowed to vote, hold political office, or act as judges or jurors. Also, most ex-slaves still had no choice but to depend on their former owners for work. This resulted in an economic system that continued to be controlled by the wealthy settlers who owned the land.

During this same period, Belize also attracted other ethnic groups. One was the Garifuna, descendants of two groups—Africans who had escaped from slavery and Carib people who inhabited the Lesser Antilles, a chain of islands in the eastern Caribbean. The Garifuna fought the British, who wanted to colonize the island chain. The British, however, defeated them and then forcibly moved them to the Bay Islands off the coast of Honduras. From there, the Garifuna immigrated to various places along the Caribbean coast, including the southern coast of Belize. In 1802 a small group of Garifuna settled in the area that is now the town of Dangriga. There, they became fishermen and farmers. The British settlers in Belize, however, treated the Garifuna as squatters, preventing them from owning land. Many of the Garifuna, therefore, ended up working for small wages as woodcutters

A modern-day descendant of the Garifuna people plays traditional music on the porch of his house in southern Belize.

alongside Creole laborers. Meanwhile, the Maya, who attacked the British logging camps and could not be subdued as a source of free labor, were forcibly removed by the British from many of their settlements. Like the Garifuna, the Maya were prevented from owning the land on which they lived.

Thus, as of the mid-nineteenth century, Belize had a mixed but highly structured society made up of a tiny group of wealthy and politically dominant white landowners, a larger group of African slave descendants called Creoles, and small communities of hostile and even more dispossessed Maya and Garifuna.

BRITISH HONDURAS

In 1862 the settlement of Belize was renamed British Honduras and was officially declared a British colony. This elevation to colonial status was preceded by changes in the settlement's government that diminished the power of the settler elite and gave Britain much greater control over the Belize area. In 1854, for example, a formal constitution was established and an elected Legislative Assembly was created to replace the Public Meeting. The legislature was made up of eighteen property owners, but the British superintendent in charge of the settlement held the real political power. He was authorized to dissolve the assembly, initiate legislation, and veto any laws that did not meet his approval.

In 1871 Britain increased its power over its colony. It approved a new constitution, abolished the Legislative Assembly, and appointed a new Legislative Council that served British interests. Under this new arrangement, the colony was governed by a governor and a council of nine appointed members.

The increases in British power during this period were partly the result of Mayan attacks on British logging camps in the interior of Belize. A war in the Yucatán in the 1840s called the Guerra de las Castas (War of the Classes) produced thousands of Mayan and Mestizo refugees, some of whom settled in western Belize just beyond the British logging frontier. In 1866 one group of Maya led by Marcos Canul attacked a mahogany camp and took prisoners. Canul demanded ransoms for the prisoners and rent for the land used by the camp. In 1870 Canul was bold enough to occupy the town of Corozal. White landowners and legislators involved in the timber industry sought protection from the attacks, but merchants along the coast who were not under attack balked at paying for the costly military expeditions. Unable to agree, the settler legislature was willing to give up political power in order to obtain security and military protection from the British government. The gamble paid off for the settlers: Canul was killed by British troops in 1872, ending the Mayan attacks, and the Mayan community was subsequently forced by the British to live on reservations.

ECONOMIC STRUGGLE

Despite its focus on trade, the colonial period slowed Belize's economy. The early economy was dominated by the forestry industry, and in the mid-1800s just a few companies, such as the powerful British Honduras Company, owned most of the land containing the valuable mahogany trees. The only other major industry at this time was production of chicle, a gum taken from the sapodilla tree that was used to make chewing gum. By the 1900s, however, both of these industries were in rapid decline. Indiscriminate logging and poor forest management had destroyed much of the region's forests, affecting the mahogany trade. Furthermore, Europe developed a new synthetic form of chicle that reduced the continent's need for Belize's chicle exports.

Besides forestry, other industries, such as agriculture, were not actively pursued, largely because timber traders dominated the legislature. In the 1850s, however, some of the big landowners who were frustrated with the declining mahogany business started sugarcane farms. In this way, the British Honduras Company, already the dominant power in the forestry industry, also became the biggest sugar producer. By 1868 over three thousand acres of land were planted in sugarcane. Still, the industry did not immediately replace the income generated by timber. Other former lumbermen tried growing bananas, coffee, cacao (the source of chocolate), and other crops, but none of these proved to be successful at the time. The economy therefore remained dependent on the timber industry.

The worldwide depression of the 1930s shattered what was left of the colony's economy. Orders for mahogany and chicle dried up even more, and large numbers of people were unemployed. Those who still found work in mahogany

THE SUGARCANE INDUSTRY IN BELIZE

Although sugarcane is an important crop in Belize today, it did not replace wood products as the country's main export until the 1960s. In 1972 large plantation farms were eliminated and small farmers became the main producers of sugarcane in Belize. The market for sugar boomed in the 1970s, and sugarcane produced good incomes for farmers. Increased global demands, however, induced Belizean farmers to expand their production, placing many of them deep in debt. In the 1980s, demand for sugar decreased, artificial sweeteners flooded the market, and sugar prices crashed, leaving many small farmers in poverty.

Today, sugarcane remains the main agricultural crop in northern Belize and the country's most important export. Although some farmers have tried to diversify their farms by growing other crops such as potatoes, onions, and corn, for most farmers sugarcane continues to be their main source of income. Growing sugarcane to the exclusion of other crops, however, prevents Belizean farmers from producing food needed to feed the people of Belize. Instead, sugarcane is sold abroad, and the money is used to import food from other countries at inflated prices. The reliance on one crop has also made the Belize economy vulnerable to international price swings.

camps often were not paid wages but instead were given rations of inferior flour and other foods by their employers. Such conditions resulted in widespread poverty, malnutrition, illness, and starvation. In 1931 economic conditions were made even worse when a major hurricane hit Belize Town, the colony's main economic center. The storm killed more than one thousand people and destroyed most of the housing. Many of the colony's inhabitants were left without a job or a place to live.

The colonial government forgave taxes and arranged for land grants and loans to rescue some of the biggest companies, but it did little to help ordinary workers. The British governor, for example, rejected proposals in 1931 that would have legalized trade unions and provided for a minimum wage and health insurance.

POLITICAL REFORM

The colony's economic difficulties and Britain's failure to react soon led to political agitation. In 1934, fed up with the hardships created by the depression and desperate for food, Belize's poor people began to demonstrate, riot, and strike for better conditions. The first of these efforts was a protest march in Belize Town on February 14, 1934. It was staged by a group known as the Unemployed Brigade, but the march sparked a broader movement, led by Antonio Soberanis Gómez, called the Labourers and Unemployed Association (LUA). Soberanis and his allies organized biweekly meetings that were attended by hundreds of people. The LUA demanded that the governor and rich merchants provide some economic help to workers and the poor.

Soberanis was jailed in 1935, but his efforts at reform succeeded in several respects. First, they forced the governor to create a program that put many people back to work in public work projects such as road building. The governor was also moved to press for a more representative legislature. Although poor people who did not own land were still not permitted to vote, by 1939 six middle-class Creoles who were more sympathetic toward labor had been elected to the Belize Town Board. In addition, labor reforms were made in the early 1940s to legalize and empower trade unions, a development that soon resulted in the General Workers' Union (GWU), a popular and colony-wide labor organization. The LUA and the GWU, in turn, supported nationalist political movements that criticized the political system and called for greater voter eligibility and the right for the people to elect the government. The colonial voting system in place at that time featured property and income standards that allowed only the wealthiest 2 percent of the population voting rights. In fact, as of 1945, only 822 voters were registered in a population of over 63,000.

The labor agitation of the 1930s, therefore, marked the beginning of a Belizean movement toward greater autonomy and independence from the British. As Bolland puts it, "The 1930s were a crucible of modern Belizean politics, a decade in which the old phenomena of exploitive labor conditions and authoritarian colonial and industrial relations began to give way to new industrial and political processes."[7] It took many more decades, however, before Belize became fully independent.

3

NATIONHOOD FOR BELIZE

The colonial exploitation of Belize and the economic conditions it created united a broad coalition of workers, poor people, and the middle class against Britain's colonial government. This movement eventually led to full independence for the country in 1981. Since then, Belize has sought to repair the legacy of poverty and underdevelopment brought about by colonial rule.

THE ROAD TO INDEPENDENCE

Independence for Belize was ultimately realized largely because of decades of agitation by the followers of one man—George Cadle Price. Price was of mixed Creole and Mayan ethnicity, a graduate of the elite St. John's College, and a member of Belize's English-speaking middle class. He had studied in and had close ties with the United States. Price began his political career in 1947 when he and several other St. John's College graduates were elected to the Belize City Council. The group soon started a newspaper, the *Belize Billboard,* to criticize colonial policies and bring attention to the needs of the poor. In addition, because of his connections with the United States, Price was a firm believer in capitalism, the economic system practiced in the United States in which businesses are owned by private individuals and are allowed to freely market and sell their goods.

Price stepped to the forefront of Belizean politics on December 31, 1949, when the British governor of British Honduras reduced the value of the colony's currency. The devaluation angered various labor groups as well as the middle class. The decision benefited large companies but led to higher prices for goods, increased unemployment, and greater poverty for many poor people. It also reminded the educated middle class of the broad reach of the colonial government's

GEORGE CADLE PRICE: BELIZE'S FOUNDING FATHER

George Cadle Price was a dominant force in Belizean politics for more than thirty-five years. Price, a product of mixed Creole and Mayan heritage, grew up in a middle-class family and attended the elite secondary school St. John's College in Belize City. In the 1930s, believing he wanted to enter the Catholic priesthood, Price studied with the Jesuits in the United States. Instead of becoming a priest, however, he returned to Belize in 1942 and became a secretary for Robert Turton, a Creole millionaire and member of the Belize Legislative Council. Soon after, Price entered politics himself.

After an unsuccessful try in 1943, Price succeeded, along with several colleagues from St. John's College, in getting elected to the Belize City Council in 1947. Shortly thereafter, he and his friends started a newspaper, the *Belize Billboard*, as a way to criticize colonial policies. This group was closely connected with the United States, and they pursued antisocialist, pro-free-enterprise, and pro-democracy policies for Belize. In later years, as head of both the People's United Party and the General Workers' Union, Price worked for decades to oust the colonial government and gain voting rights for Belizeans. His efforts eventually led to independence for Belize in 1981, and Price became the nation's very first prime minister.

Britain's Prince Michael (right) transfers power to Prime Minister Price during a ceremony to mark Belize's independence in 1981.

power. Thus on the same night of the devaluation decision, a People's Committee was formed that united laborers, the poor, and the middle class against colonial rule. A short while later, in 1950, the People's Committee was replaced by a new organization, the People's United Party (PUP). Price became PUP's secretary, and his newspaper colleagues were prominent PUP members. PUP was strongly supported by the main organization representing working people, the General Workers' Union (GWU), and Price also became the president of the GWU. This gave him even more influence.

PUP became a powerful political force as it pushed for representative government in British Honduras and eventually for independence from Britain. PUP advocated universal suffrage that would give all adults the right to vote, regardless of whether they could read and write. It also fought for true representative government. Threatened by PUP's actions and demands, the colonial government responded by dissolving the Belize City Council and by sentencing two of Price's *Billboard* colleagues to eighteen months in prison on charges of sedition. Their imprisonment, however, left Price as the leader of PUP, a position that he used to his advantage.

In 1952 PUP supported a GWU labor strike against colonial business interests. This decision cemented PUP's reputation as the champion of the colony's working people. PUP's influence also succeeded in getting the colonial government to enact reforms in 1954. The government drafted a new constitution and instituted a new Legislative Assembly consisting of nine elected members (together with three nominated and three official members). Also, most importantly, the government granted universal voting rights. PUP then advanced candidates for the colony's legislature. In the April 28, 1954, elections, in which 70 percent of the registered electorate voted, PUP candidates won eight of the nine elected seats in the Legislative Assembly.

For decades thereafter, PUP won every general election and almost all local elections, crushing all opposition candidates. During these years, the group directed all its efforts toward one goal: developing popular support for full independence from Britain. PUP held classes and sponsored other educational events, both in Belize City and in rural areas, and, despite some infighting among its leaders, managed to mobilize working people throughout the colony.

By 1961 Britain was finally convinced that it should allow the colony to become more independent. The turning point was a 1960 constitutional conference held in London. PUP joined forces with opposition political groups to present a united front at the conference in favor of self-government for British Honduras. The British government agreed with many of these demands, and the colony's constitution was changed to expand the number of elected legislative seats to eighteen. In 1964 the constitution was changed once again to create a government consisting of a governor, a cabinet led by a prime minister, an independent judiciary, and a bicameral (two-house) legislature with an elected house of representatives and an appointed senate. This government was given complete control over virtually all internal matters in Belize. Britain, however, maintained control over matters such as internal security, foreign policy, and defense.

During the next decade, support for PUP declined as a new generation of political activists gained power in the colony. These activists included more radical and younger men such as Said Musa, Evan Hyde, and Assad Shoman. At the same time, PUP lost support in the business community and struggled with economic problems. Ultimately, however, these developments led to a two-party system with two main political parties, PUP and the United Democratic Party

In 1978 a British soldier stationed in Belize to protect it from a Guatemalan invasion chats with local children. The dispute between the two countries dates to the 1700s.

(UDP). UDP was formed in 1973 when three opposition parties combined into one entity that began to win some elections against PUP leadership. As scholar Ian Peedle explains, UDP "managed, with the support of the Belize business community, to establish itself as the only effective opposition to the PUP."[8] PUP and UDP competed for power in Belize in the 1970s, but they both sought independence from Britain.

THE GUATEMALA DISPUTE AND INDEPENDENCE

In these later years, the main obstacle to independence actually was not Britain but a claim on the area by the neighboring country of Guatemala. Indeed, during this time Britain began taking steps to prepare the colony for independence. For example, the colony's name was changed on June 1, 1973, to Belize, and beginning in 1975, Britain allowed the colonial government to participate in international diplomacy.

The dispute with Guatemala arose from the confusion over Spain and Britain's competing claims for the area of Belize in the 1700s and 1800s. The two countries during that period had negotiated treaties that allowed British settlements but at the same time affirmed Spanish sovereignty. When the Spanish empire in Central America disintegrated in the 1820s, one of the independent countries that emerged, Guatemala, claimed that it had inherited Spain's sovereign rights over the Belize area. In 1859 Britain and Guatemala tried to resolve this dispute with a treaty, the Anglo-Guatemalan Treaty. The treaty called for the building of a road through Belize that would link Guatemala with the Caribbean coast. Guatemala considered the road the price it should be paid to give up its claims on Belize. This road was never built, however, and in 1945 the Guatemalan government declared Belize part of Guatemala.

Britain made repeated attempts thereafter to resolve the dispute. Talks between Britain and Guatemala in 1961, 1969, and 1973, however, all ended in deadlock and in increasing tensions between Belize and Guatemala. Guatemala even threatened to invade Belize at one point, causing the British to send a large number of troops to the colony. Belize's fears of military action from Guatemala delayed its march toward independence. As Bolland explains, "[Belize's] problem of trying to eliminate all traces of residual colonialism [was] exacerbated by its continued dependence upon British forces for defense against Guatemala."[9]

In 1976, frustrated with the unwillingness of Guatemala's military leaders to resolve matters with Belize, Britain and the Belize government devised a new strategy of trying to win international support for Belizean independence. Over the next few years, Belizean leaders presented their case before several international meetings, including meetings of the United Nations. Guatemala was eventually isolated as other countries, including Latin American countries, declared their support for an independent Belize. Finally, in November 1980, the UN passed a resolution that demanded independence for Belize no later than the end of 1981.

Belize made one last attempt to reach an agreement with Guatemala prior to independence. During the talks, however, Guatemala refused Belize's proposals and withdrew from negotiations. Thus, Belize became independent on September 21, 1981, without an agreement with Guatemala. Despite the continuing threat from Guatemala, Belizeans were overjoyed. Bolland describes the scene in Belize: "The independence ceremonies and celebrations took place in a carnival atmosphere, witnessed by prominent leaders and diplomatic representatives from all over the world. . . . Delegations from [sixty-one countries] joined with musicians and dancers to celebrate."[10]

The New Belizean Government

The government that emerged in Belize reflected the country's colonial roots. As scholar Steven R. Harper explains, "Belize [became] a constitutional monarchy with a parliamentary form of government based on the British model."[11] The ceremonial head of state is a governor-general (who represents the queen of England), but real political power is held by a prime minister, a cabinet, and a legislature called the National Assembly, which is made up of a democratically elected house of representatives and an appointed senate. The constitution also provides for an independent judiciary, including a supreme court, a court of appeal, and a magistrate court in each district of the country.

According to the precise terms of the constitution, the governor-general, who is appointed by the queen, appoints the prime minister and the rest of the cabinet as well as

many senators. Although this suggests that the governor-general is very powerful, the reality is that most of the power is held by representatives elected by the people. Twenty-nine representatives are elected for five-year terms from six electoral districts—Belize, Cayo, Corozal, Orange Walk, Stann Creek, and Toledo. All Belizean adults at least eighteen years old have a right to vote in the elections. Also, under the constitution, the real head of government, the prime minister, must be chosen from the house of representatives and must have the support of the majority of house members. Typically, this post is awarded to the leader of the party that won the majority of the votes in the elections. The prime minister then chooses the rest of the cabinet members; often, those chosen are also elected representatives who must answer to voters to remain in office. In addition, the prime minister usually controls the senate, because six of the ten senators are chosen by the prime minister. Another three are selected by the opposition party, and one is picked by a group of church and business leaders.

Banners hanging above a busy street in downtown Belize City celebrate the nation's independence from Britain in 1981.

The cabinet is the main policy-making body, and it originates much of the legislation in Belize. Under the constitution, however, legislation must be approved by both houses of the National Assembly in order to become law. Because the cabinet, the house of representatives, and the senate are often made up of members of the majority party, legislation proposed by the cabinet usually stands a good chance of passing in the legislature. This system of government thus fuses two government functions—the legislative (the house and senate) and the executive (the prime minister and the cabinet). Such a system contrasts with the more republican form of government in the United States, which provides for a sharper division between executive, legislative, and judicial functions.

Belize, however, has been praised by many as a bastion of peace and democracy in Central America. In 1984, when Belize held its first successful elections after independence, for example, the *New York Times* recorded, "This tiny nation, a haven of calm amid the turmoil of Central America, holds the first general elections since independence three years ago. By regional standards, it was an uneventful campaign. No one has been barred from taking part; none of the parties has threatened a boycott, and no one has been shot or made to disappear."[12] Indeed, since its independence, Belize has experienced no military coups or election violence, and has successfully transferred power through many election cycles.

POLITICS AND ELECTIONS IN THE NEW NATION

Many observers have concluded that the elections since Belize's independence have shown that the nation is committed to democracy and peaceful changes in leadership. After independence, George Price, leader of PUP, became the country's first prime minister. PUP, however, was soon challenged by Belize's other main political party, UDP. The two parties have similar policies, but UDP is generally considered a bit more conservative and business oriented than PUP and has closer ties with the United States. In the first set of elections after independence, UDP won an overwhelming majority of the seats in the house of representatives. UDP leader Manuel Esquivel thus became Belize's second prime minister.

UDP's victory in 1984 was attributed by some to the party's focus on economic issues. Belize's economy was in bad shape at the time of independence, and the country was forced to get a loan from the International Monetary Fund

(IMF). Between 1984 and 1989, the UDP implemented an economic stabilization plan in order to obtain a loan from the IMF. This plan sought to put Belize's economy on a more solid footing by reducing government spending and raising taxes. Although the economy began to grow, the plan resulted in increases in unemployment and difficulties for the poor, because government jobs and services were cut. During the next elections, PUP criticized these results, as well as UDP policies favoring foreign investment, as damaging to Belize. In a small country like Belize, personalities are also important and Esquivel was perceived by many as arrogant, rather than a man of the people. As a result of these and other issues, Esquivel was narrowly defeated in 1989 by PUP.

UDP won again in the elections of 1993 when defense issues were at stake. Britain announced that year that it would

A 2003 election billboard in Belize City endorses the PUP candidate, Said Musa, who was elected Belize's third prime minister in 1998.

withdraw its remaining troops from Belize, and UDP campaigned by encouraging fears about the troop withdrawal. PUP, however, returned to power with a landslide victory in the 1998 elections, led by a new PUP candidate, Said Musa, who became Belize's third prime minister. Musa, a British-educated lawyer and longtime PUP activist, had become leader of PUP following George Price's retirement in 1996. PUP won the elections based on its promises to reform the Belize government by dispersing political power and by providing more checks and balances among government branches. Musa remains a popular leader in the new millennium; in the 2003 elections, he became the first person in Belizean history to win a second consecutive term as prime minister.

SAID MUSA, BELIZE'S PRIME MINISTER

Belize's third prime minister, Said Wilbert Musa, was born to a poor Palestinian Arab family in the small, rural town of San Ignacio, Belize, on March 19, 1944. Musa quickly learned the value of education. He completed primary school in San Ignacio, studied at St. Michael's College and St. John's College in Belize City, and obtained a law degree from Manchester University in England. He married, started a family, and returned to Belize in 1967 to work in public service and later a private law practice.

Eager to participate in the development of Belize, Musa became friends with political activists such as Assad Shoman and Evan Hyde. In 1974 he joined the People's United Party to help in the struggle for independence. Although Musa lost in the 1974 legislative elections, PUP leader George Price appointed him senator for the 1974–1979 term. Musa decisively won in the 1979 elections and returned to the legislature. Later, Musa was appointed to the positions of attorney general, minister of education and sports, and minister for economic development. He also traveled extensively, representing Belize at regional and international forums.

Musa helped draft the country's constitution just before independence was achieved in 1981 and served as foreign minister for the new country. In 1996 he became the leader of PUP when George Price resigned. Musa was elected prime minister in 1998 and was reelected for a second term in 2003. His popularity has been attributed to his warm and compassionate personality, great listening skills, and masterful public-speaking abilities. Many in Belize view him as a man of vision and action and a very effective leader.

Prime Minister Musa speaks at a conference of Caribbean nations in February 2002. Musa is well known for his public-speaking abilities.

THE BELIZEAN ECONOMY

Today, Belize is struggling to escape its colonial past and find its place in the world economy. Its economy has historically been based on trade, and during its early years, Belize was dependent almost completely on the export of timber. The forestry industry, however, never recovered from the depression of the 1930s. Also, centuries of British exploitation largely depleted Belize of much of its valuable timber. The loss of the timber industry forced Belize to shift to other industries and products. During the 1960s and 1970s, agricultural products, primarily sugar, became the country's leading exports, and the country's economy grew rapidly.

A dramatic drop in worldwide sugar prices in 1984, however, combined with some other factors to create an economic crisis for Belize. Suddenly, the country was importing many more goods than it was exporting, creating a huge trade deficit. This crisis was the trigger that led to the IMF loan and economic reform program. The program, however difficult for Belizeans, succeeded in improving the country's economy by the end of the 1980s.

ECOTOURISM IN BELIZE

Belize's pristine environment—its barrier reef, rain forests, and mountain caves—makes the country a very attractive spot for tourists seeking to experience the unspoiled wonders of nature. The country's warm tropical weather, vibrant culture, and Mayan ruins add to its attraction for tourists. For many other Central American countries, however, the creation of a tourism industry has meant the unchecked development of large luxury resorts and hotels to attract as many tourists as possible. This approach, unfortunately, can easily lead to destruction of the natural environment, the very habitat that first attracted such tourism. In the 1980s, Belize recognized that it could promote a different type of tourism industry, one that would focus on small-scale hotels and resorts with the overriding goal of protecting environmental riches. Ecotourism, as it is called, has been very successful for Belize: It now provides the largest share of the country's foreign revenues.

Two ecotourists enjoy a boat excursion along Belize's Monkey River.

Stung by the sugar crisis, Belize has worked to diversify its economy in order to become less affected by financial downturns when one sector of its economy becomes sluggish. One way it has done this is by promoting growth in other agricultural exports besides sugar. Today, bananas and citrus fruits such as oranges and grapefruit are staple crops for the country. Belize also has focused on exporting seafood, primarily lobsters, conch, and shrimp. This industry has become an important income producer. Another new focus for the country is the reexport trade, which involves importing goods into Belize and then selling them to neighboring countries. As for manufacturing, there are only a few factories in Belize, and they make products mainly for the local market, such as flour, furniture, beer and soft drinks, cigarettes, shoes and clothing, and matches. The most promising new industry is ecotourism, which attracts tourists to Belize to see and explore its protected natural environment. The country clearly has much to offer tourists, from its remarkable barrier reef to its pristine rain forest preserves and Mayan ruins. Indeed, tourism has now eclipsed sugarcane as the main source of revenue for Belize.

BELIZE'S FOREIGN RELATIONS

Since independence, Belize has maintained a close relationship with Britain for several practical reasons. First, given the ongoing threat from Guatemala, Belize needed to rely on Britain for military defense. Britain maintained fifteen hundred troops in Belize to guarantee the country's security and provided other military aid. All permanent troops were withdrawn in 1994, but Belize has continued to depend on Britain for other assistance. For example, Britain provided Belize with grants of about $1.4 million per year in the early 1990s and $13.5 million in interest-free loans between 1989 and 1994. Valuable trade preferences given to Belize by Britain are yet another critical link between the two countries.

Belize has sought to expand its foreign relationships beyond Britain, however. Today, its strongest foreign ally is the United States. The relationship began even before independence, when leaders of the anticolonial movement sought U.S. ties as a way to escape total dependence on Britain. Since independence, both PUP and UDP leaders have consistently

A sign on Belize's border with Guatemala celebrates its sovereignty. Guatemala did not recognize Belize as an independent nation until 1991.

promoted alliances with the United States and have tried to model its free-market economic policies. The United States has responded favorably to Belize in order to promote democracy, find new business markets, and control drug trafficking in Central America. Like Britain, the United States has been generous in providing aid to Belize. Although aid has been declining in recent years, in the 1980s and 1990s, U.S. economic assistance averaged around $10 million per year. Also like Britain, the United States has been a valuable trading partner to Belize. In 2000, for example, the United States exported $32 million in agricultural products to the country, while consuming about $67 million of Belizean goods, primarily sugar and bananas.

Over time, Belize has also become closer to its Central American neighbors, including Guatemala. Relations with Guatemala began to improve in 1985, when Guatemala adopted a new constitution that did not include its historical claims to Belize. Following a series of negotiations, Guatemala officially recognized Belize as an independent country on August 14, 1991. Belize responded by allowing Guatemalans access to international waters from the Belize coast, and the two countries established diplomatic relations in September 1991. Although these relations continue to be rocky, the effort has reduced the military threat from Guatemala.

With regard to other countries in Central America and beyond, Belize has continued to reach out, as it did while seeking independence, to participate in regional and international organizations. For example, Belize is a member of the World Trade Organization (WTO), an international trade organization, as well as regional associations such as the Caribbean Community and Common Market (CARICOM), a trade organization of Caribbean countries, and the Organization of American States (OAS), a group of Western Hemisphere countries devoted to democracy and trade. Belize has close trade relations with Mexico and Venezuela, in particular, and has made China its third biggest trading partner. Under Prime Minister Musa, the country also has begun to take a much more active role in the UN and international affairs.

Although small and still newly independent, and with much work still necessary to stabilize its economy and security, Belize clearly has made great strides away from its colonial roots.

4

THE PEOPLE OF BELIZE

The rich diversity of Belize's population is rooted in its colonial past. Today, descendants of British settlers and African slaves still form the cultural and economic elite. Yet they mix with descendants of Mayan natives as well as with numerous immigrants from throughout the Caribbean and Central America. Together, the people are a mosaic of different races, cultures, languages, and religions. Although Belize is proud of this diversity, the country struggles with another legacy of its colonial past—a pattern of continuing economic inequalities among its different races and classes.

THE CREOLES, THE MESTIZOS, AND THE MAYA

The society of Belize has a multitude of different ethnic groups. One of the largest and most influential groups is the

These children, living in San Miguel in southern Belize, are direct descendants of the ancient Maya. The Maya comprise Belize's third largest ethnic group.

Creoles, an English-speaking people descended largely from European settlers and African slaves who were imported to work in Belize's early mahogany industry. Male slaves usually lived in remote mahogany camps, but female slaves often lived in servant quarters in British settlements, and they sometimes bore children fathered by white masters. Some of these children were freed by their fathers, contributing to a growing free colored population, some of whom became educated and wealthy. After the abolition of slavery, full-blooded African blacks also became free. This interrelationship among whites, slaves, and free colored people produced a racially mixed Creole culture, including some people with dark skin and African hair and features and others with very light skin and European features. As Belize moved toward independence, Creoles came to dominate Belizean culture, politics, and economic life. In fact, a few wealthy and influential families who are direct descendants of white settlers still form the top elite of Belizean society. Creoles, therefore, have historically considered themselves as the most authentic Belizean culture. At the same time, however, they make up only about 25 percent of the population, and most live in or around Belize City.

Surrounding the Creole society in Belize City is a Spanish-speaking Mestizo population of mixed Hispanic and American Indian origins. The Mestizos make up almost half of the total population of Belize. As Ian Peedle notes, "It is all too easy to imagine Belize City as an island of Caribbean Creole culture in an Hispanic sea."[13] Many Mestizos are descendants of refugees who fled to Belize from the Yucatán during the Guerra de las Castas in the mid-1800s. Other Mestizos are part of a wave of newer immigrants from various neighboring Central American countries that were plagued by civil wars during the 1980s. Most Mestizos have settled in northern towns such as Corozal and Orange Walk; in western towns such as San Ignacio, Santa Elena, and Benque Viejo; or in villages in southern Belize. This infusion of Spanish-speaking people into Belize has greatly affected Belizean culture. According to Peedle, "The obvious signs include the Latino music played in clubs and on the radio and the restaurants serving Hispanic foods such as burritos, tacos, and garnaches [fried corn tortillas topped with beans, cabbage, and cheese]."[14]

Two Mestizo girls stand outside their mother's produce market in San Pedro, Belize. Mestizos make up nearly half of the country's population.

The third largest ethnic group in Belize is the Maya, a population formed from three distinct subgroups. Two of these subgroups—the Kekchí and Mopán—are mostly descendants of Maya who emigrated from Guatemala and settled in northern Belize in the late nineteenth century. A third subgroup is the Yucatec Maya, who are primarily descendants of the ancient Maya scattered in rural villages throughout the south. Many Maya are poor and still live, as they always have, in remote communities made up of small, thatched houses where they grow their own food and raise chickens and pigs to survive.

THE GARIFUNA, THE MENNONITES, AND OTHER ETHNIC GROUPS

Belize is also home to several other distinct ethnic groups. One is the Garifuna, descendants of African slaves who intermarried with American Indians from the eastern Caribbean islands and settled the southern Belizean coasts

THE MENNONITES

Belize is home to a thriving population of Mennonites, a group of white settlers who are members of the Mennonite Church. The church was founded in Zurich, Switzerland, in 1525 by Menno Simons. Simons was a Dutchman who later moved his followers to Holland. Mennonites believe that religion must be separate from the State and that theirs is the true Christian faith. They are avid pacifists—that is, people who reject all violence and war. As a group, the Mennonites have often suffered persecution because of their pacifist beliefs, causing them to search for new places to live where they could be left in peace.

In the 1950s, many migrated to Belize. There, their Mennonite lifestyle makes them stand out from other Belizeans. Mennonites wear old-fashioned clothing—ankle-length dresses and hats for women and bib overalls for men—and some insist on avoiding modern conveniences such as electricity, cars, and technology. They can often be seen riding in horse-pulled buggies, and they tend to segregate themselves from the rest of society, organizing their own schools and social activities. Despite their segregation, the Mennonites have been an asset for the Belizean economy. They tend to be highly efficient produce and dairy farmers, and they have developed many parts of the Belize countryside into profit-making agricultural enterprises.

A group of young Mennonite men take a break along a dirt road in Belize.

in the early 1800s. Today, Belize's Garifuna population continues to be concentrated in the south around Dangriga. Most of the people here are fishermen, farmers, or government employees.

Another important ethnic group is the Mennonites, an all-white religious group with roots in Holland. The first group of Mennonites to migrate to Belize came from Mexico in 1958 and settled in western Belize. Today, however, the Mennonites have spread throughout the country and have developed a reputation as successful produce and dairy farmers.

Several smaller ethnic groups, including East Indians, Europeans, Chinese, and Arabs, make up the rest of Belize's population. The East Indians are descendants of indentured laborers who were brought to Belize in the 1800s to work on sugar plantations. Most of them have intermarried with other ethnic groups. Belize's Arabs are Palestinians who immigrated to Belize in the late 1800s and early 1900s. Similarly, some Chinese immigrated to the country in the early twentieth century, supplemented by a wave of newer immigrants from Hong Kong and Taiwan in the late 1980s. A small, white community of British and American expatriates and international aid workers also live in Belize.

The divisions between Belize's ethnic groups are not clearly defined. Although some groups such as the Mennonites and some Maya remain segregated, members of most ethnic groups have interacted and intermarried over the years. This has produced a highly complex society in which many Belizeans are a mix of numerous ethnic and cultural strains. Adding to the complexity are racial, language, social, class, and religious factors that often cross ethnic lines. As a result, some people no longer identify with any particular ethnic label. As scholar Charles Rutheiser explains, "A small, but significant number of people [avoid] potentially divisive ethnic categories and [refer] to themselves simply as 'Belizeans.'"[15]

IMMIGRATION AND EMIGRATION

Belize's ethnic diversity illustrates that it is a country of immigrants. Its population is made up of different peoples who immigrated to Belize throughout its history. Today, Belize continues to attract immigrants, primarily from neighboring countries such as Mexico, El Salvador, Honduras, and Guatemala. The number of Belizeans from these areas was estimated to be about 10 to 20 percent of the population in the 1980s, and this number has increased dramatically since then.

These Central American immigrants have moved into Belize's countryside and have changed the country from a primarily urban one to one in which the majority of the population lives in rural areas. Most of the new immigrants are poor, and they create a significant burden for the Belize government as it tries to provide assistance, jobs, and services for them. Moreover, the immigration has enlarged the gulf between urban and rural life in Belize. Rural residents often live lives of poverty while urban Belizeans generally have a higher standard of living.

Immigration, combined with a high birthrate and improved health care that has increased infant survival rates, has also caused an increase in the overall population of Belize and has produced an essentially youthful Belizean society. As of 2004, more than 40 percent of Belizeans were under the age of fourteen, and the median age of the population was about nineteen years old. At the same time, improved health care has decreased the death rate in Belize, increasing the number of older citizens. Even with the recent population increases, however, Belize remains one of the most sparsely populated countries in Central America.

Alongside this immigration into the country, an increasing number of Belizeans are leaving the country to live in other nations—primarily the United States—where better and higher-paying jobs can be found. Those leaving tend to be English-speaking Creoles and Garifuna from Belize's urban areas. This emigration has reduced the country's urban population at the same time that Spanish-speaking immi-

Members of an immigrant family pose in the doorway of their house along Belize's Monkey River. Most of the country's immigrant population lives in rural areas.

grants have been populating rural areas and adding to the country's Spanish-speaking majority. These trends have caused some ethnic tensions because many Creoles and other English speakers resent the growing Latino culture and its challenge to Creole dominance. As Rutheiser explains, the changes have "challenged long-held assumptions regarding the character of Belizean culture, which has traditionally been oriented toward the English-speaking Caribbean."[16]

LANGUAGES

Despite the recent influx of Hispanics, standard English is the official language of Belize and the language taught in its schools. According to the 1991 census, English also is the most widely spoken language in Belize. A large number of English speakers, however, speak a local version of English called Creole. Creole is actually a mixture of English and African words and grammar, and it is often hard for even native English speakers to understand. The Creole language developed among African slaves during colonial times as a way for them to communicate among themselves and keep African culture alive despite attempts by white settlers to impose European culture on them. Today, Creole English is the predominant language of Belizeans, especially in the Belize City area. Many also speak standard English, but, as Peedle notes, "Creole is the language of the street."[17]

Another one-third to one-half of the population speaks Spanish as their primary language. The number of Spanish speakers, however, is increasing as new immigrants arrive from other places in Central America. Still other languages in Belize include Garifuna, three different Mayan languages, German (spoken by the Mennonites), and Hindi (spoken by a few East Indian immigrants).

An increasing number of people speak at least two languages, largely because many Spanish, Mayan, and Garifuna speakers also speak the standard English taught in school. Some Belizeans are even trilingual. A number of Garifuna, for example, speak English and Spanish in addition to their own language.

RELIGION

The diversity apparent in ethnic groups and languages is also seen in religious affiliation in Belize. Most Belizeans are

Roman Catholic due to the influence of Spain in Central and South America. The first Catholic church in Belize was built in 1851 by refugees from the Yucatán. As years passed, the Catholic religion was adopted by many Creole people, as well as a number of Maya and Garifuna. The popularity of the religion stems, in part, from the fact that early churches offered social and educational services along with instruction in the Catholic faith. Indeed, Belize's most prestigious school—St. John's College in Belize City—is a Catholic school. Today, Catholicism crosses all ethnic lines and has become one of the country's strongest institutions.

Because of the early British presence, a large number of Protestant religions are also active in Belize. These include Anglican (also called the Church of England), Methodist, Presbyterian, and Seventh-Day Adventist. Modern American missionaries have also introduced evangelical religions to the country, including sects such as Assemblies of God, Baptists, Mormons, and Jehovah's Witnesses. In addition, Mennonites are a growing force. Finally, several non-Christian religions have a few followers. These include Islam, Hinduism, Judaism, and the Baha'i Faith.

CLASS DIVISIONS

A less desirable aspect of Belize's colonial legacy is a glaring economic inequality among its various ethnic groups. During colonial times, a small group of white settlers, together with some freed slaves, dominated Belize. Decades after independence, a small elite of whites, light-skinned Creoles, and some Mestizos still controls most of the political and economic power in the country. Members of this group own many of the country's commercial, retail, and manufacturing businesses and hold the most prominent professional and governmental positions. Most live near the ocean in Belize City, share the Catholic faith, and enjoy the same social clubs and activities. Typically, this elite group also receives the best schooling. Many children from this group attend prestigious universities in Britain or the United States.

Belize also has a sizable middle class largely made up of owners of small businesses, professionals, teachers, skilled manual tradespersons, and government workers. The middle class embodies all ethnic groups—Creoles, Mestizos, Garifuna, and others. Many from this economic group are

FOLK BELIEFS IN BELIZE

Folk beliefs and superstitions are a common part of the culture in Belize. For example, many Belizean children grow up hearing about *El Duende*, a mythical evil dwarf said to be about three feet tall. *El Duende* is easy to recognize because he has no thumbs. He lives in the forest and punishes children who kill animals or do other mischief there. Another legend tells the story of *El Sisimito*, a hairy gorilla-like beast similar to the Sasquatch of North America. *El Sisimito* has his feet on backwards and has no knees. He is said to feast on humans and is afraid of only water and dogs. Yet another folk tale features *X'tabai*, a beautiful woman of Indian descent with long, silky black hair who lures men into the forest. There, *X'tabai* makes love to her victim, who afterward may die of fever. Only by making the sign of the cross can men make *X'tabai* disappear before she can cast her spell.

Many other superstitions in Belize are associated with Good Friday. On that day, many Belizeans avoid swimming in the sea or rivers, they set eggs in glasses to see the future, and they look for flowers on the ruda plant to bring good fortune. Other folk beliefs of the Garifuna involve the *gubida*, the spirits of ancestors, who can be called on to help solve problems of the living. These spirits are contacted by *buyeis*, or spirit helpers, through the use of witchcraft, rituals, and ceremonies.

Belizeans who benefited from the increased educational and employment opportunities provided by the government in the second half of the twentieth century. Still, ethnic identity often influenced such opportunities. Creoles, for example, typically became entrenched in the skilled trades and in professions such as law and accounting, while Mestizos and Garifuna tended to find employment in government or teaching jobs, small businesses, or farming. Despite the fact that they are educated and skilled, however, some middle-class Belizeans have faced very limited job prospects in Belize, causing many to move to the United States.

By far the largest economic class in Belize is the poor, who form a majority of the population. A large number of poor people live in urban areas such as Belize City. Some of the poorest, however, reside in rustic and isolated rural villages, where services and government help are often unavailable.

They face much more limited educational and economic opportunities than the middle class. Many are unemployed, and most of those who are employed work as temporary unskilled laborers, low-paid agricultural workers, or subsistence farmers. The majority of poor families lack the financial ability to send their children to school beyond the primary level. This decreases the chances of future generations obtaining better jobs and raising their prospects. Experts have linked the lack of educational and economic opportunities to dramatic increases in illegal drugs, street gang warfare, and crime in recent decades in Belize. Indeed, unemployment, escalating violent crime, and drugs are some of the country's most pressing social problems today.

GOVERNMENT SOCIAL SERVICES

To address some of the problems of poverty in Belize, the government provides education, health care, and other social benefits. The school system in Belize was started by churches, and today it is a mixture of religious and state-run schools. Still, most schools are run by churches. In recent years, however, the number of state-run primary and secondary schools has grown and the country now has a state-run college, the University College of Belize (UCB). The state has also created vocational and adult education centers. Under Belizean law, primary and secondary education is free, but families are expected to pay for schoolbooks and other school expenses such as laboratory and activity fees. The government also provides students with aid for postsecondary schools based on good grades and merit.

Education is compulsory for children between the ages of six and fourteen. Many children, however, drop out of school before age fourteen, either because their parents cannot afford school expenses or because they need to work to help support their families. Only a minority manage to complete secondary school, and even fewer attend colleges or postsecondary vocational schools. Since at least a secondary education is needed to get a skilled job in Belize, the failure to acquire educational credentials condemns many in Belize to a life of poverty. The quality of education is another problem. Class sizes tend to be large, particularly in rural areas, where two classes are sometimes combined, and less than 50 percent of Belizean teachers are properly trained.

As with education, Belize's government has made improvements in health care since colonial times. Today, three indicators of health show vast improvement from past statistics: Death rates have been reduced from 11.5 per 1,000 in the 1950s to 6.04 deaths per 1,000 in 2004; infant mortality has declined from 93 per 1,000 in the 1950s to 26.37 deaths per 1,000 in 2004; and life expectancy is now estimated at more than 67 years. Most Belizeans are now provided health care by eight government hospitals and numerous clinics. Specialty facilities provide maternal, child care, and dental services. Water and sewage systems also have been improved over the years to prevent diseases caused by unclean water and improper sanitation. Nutrition education programs have helped ensure that people eat healthier foods.

Still, quality-of-care issues remain. Hospitals and other care facilities outside of Belize City often lack modern equipment and medicines, and there is a constant shortage of qualified doctors, nurses, and dentists. Diseases such as malaria, dengue fever (another mosquito-borne disease), and AIDS are on the increase, and malnutrition continues to be a problem for a significant number of Belizean children, particularly children of new immigrants to the country. In addition, although rural and mobile clinics serve the countryside, many of the poor who live in isolated rural areas still lack access to health care.

Christian schoolgirls take a class trip to a park in Belize City. Most schools in Belize are run by churches.

WOMEN IN BELIZE

Although the roles of Belizean women vary among the country's many ethnic groups, women in Belize generally do not have the same opportunities and civil rights as men. Many poorer women still do difficult and unpaid work in the home as wives and mothers. For poorer families, women's home duties are often very labor intensive due to the lack of electricity or in-house plumbing and the unavailability of markets or shops. In one study conducted among the Maya, for example, women reported that they spent as much as ninety hours per week doing household tasks such as preparing meals, washing clothes, taking care of children, and helping their spouses with farm tasks.

For those women lucky enough to find paid work, life is not that much better. Most women work in manual labor or service industries under terrible working conditions, and they earn even lower wages than the men in those industries. In addition, some women face domestic violence—physical and sexual abuse by their husbands or boyfriends that is often ignored by the police and justice system.

Women's groups in Belize, however, are challenging these conditions. In 1991 the first female labor union, the Women's Workers Union (WWU), was created, and it played a vital role in enacting the country's first minimum-wage law in 1992. Other successes include the creation of family court to help women get child support and the passing of a 1993 domestic violence bill designed to help women confront physical abuse. In the years to come, women in Belize are expected to become even more empowered.

A mother and her daughters prepare tortillas in a traditional Mayan home.

The Belizean government has also undertaken other efforts to better the lives of its citizens. After independence, for example, the government increased the number of government and civil service jobs, hiring many educated Belizeans for jobs in professional-level occupations. In addition, as of 1981, the government began providing a program of social security benefits. The program provides cash benefits to workers who become unable to work because of sickness, maternity, retirement, or workplace injury.

HOUSING

Housing in Belize mirrors the economic diversity found in Belizean society. Most houses are constructed of wooden clapboards, but styles and sizes vary greatly depending on social and economic factors. For example, in places like Belize City, the elite often live in colonial mansions or oceanfront houses that feature grand staircases, numerous rooms, glass windows, and balconies or verandas where people can sit and enjoy the ocean breezes. Most houses for the poor and working class, meanwhile, are unpainted, rundown shacks. These dwellings may have two or three rooms, tin roofs, and wooden shutters instead of windows. Along the coast, many of these houses are built on stilts or set on concrete blocks to keep them dry during storms. Yet most homes, especially those in or near cities, at least have indoor water, toilets, and electricity. In poorer areas in rural Belize, however, many houses are built from mud or wood with thatched or palm roofs and have no indoor plumbing or electricity.

The government in recent years has sought to improve housing conditions. In fact, the centerpiece of the country's efforts to combat poverty has been a program to construct ten thousand new low-income houses throughout the country between 1998 and 2003. This program put many Belizeans to work on construction projects, helping to reduce unemployment and create thousands of new homes.

Despite the various efforts by the government to provide education, health care, housing, and jobs, however, Belize continues to be plagued by high levels of poverty, unemployment, and substandard living conditions. More than one-third of Belizeans live in poverty, most of them in southern and rural Belize. The government estimates that the unemployment rate has been reduced from 14.3 percent in 1999 to about 9.1 percent in 2003, but critics think it is much higher.

Although solid improvements have been made in the years since independence, Belize still has a long way to go to provide all its people with economic opportunity and a comfortable life.

5

CULTURE AND LIFESTYLE

Culture in Belize is a product of Belize's colonial past and its diverse ethnic mix. In addition, the nation's culture is greatly influenced by Belize's location at the crossroads of Central America and the Caribbean. Perhaps the strongest influences in recent years, however, are the nation's growing tourist industry and its strong ties to the United States, both of which bring American ideas, images, and consumer goods into Belize.

CULTURAL INFLUENCES

With its ethnically diverse society, multiple regional influences, and history of European development, Belize has a rich mix of languages, beliefs, and customs. Since independence, Belize's government has been focused on the economy and other critical nation-building issues and has not been able to fund the arts or otherwise encourage positive aspects of Belizean culture. As a result, many art forms and cultural traditions are only just developing in Belize.

Belize is also bombarded by foreign images and culture, an influence that further dilutes local art traditions. Radio stations, cable television, and videos are all now widely available in the country, bringing imported music, programs, and movies to people who previously were exposed only to local culture. American entertainment is particularly sought after, and U.S. consumer goods make up a large percentage of the country's imports. Growing numbers of American tourists and expatriates increase the U.S. influence in Belize. As sociology professor O. Nigel Bolland explains, "[American] culture has considerable economic and political support and penetrates the media and educational institutions in ways that help form the attitudes, tastes, and values of Belizeans."[18]

Recently, however, there have been signs of a revival in Belize's local arts. The government has established an arts council to support the arts, and it has attracted international funding that has been used, in part, to hold a National Children's Festival of Arts each year since 1992. Belize also has a national dance company, formed in 1991, and plans for other art organizations. St. John's College has even started an art program to train aspiring artists. In addition, the tourist industry has had a positive effect for local artists: Galleries and souvenir shops have emerged to sell arts and crafts products to visiting tourists.

LITERATURE AND PRINT MEDIA

Perhaps the most developed area of the arts in Belize is its literature. The country has two local publishing houses, the Angelus Press and Cubola, that promote Belizean writers. Angelus Press boasts that it provides the largest selection of publications and videotapes about Belize, as well as forty fiction titles. Cubola mainly focuses on books about Belize's history, environment, and literature.

The first Belizean novelist to win international recognition was Zee Edgell, a writer who features women as central

A banner hanging in Ambergris Cay announces the area's annual Halloween party. Much of Belizean life is influenced by American popular culture.

CREOLE PROVERBS

The Creole language is a kind of pidgin English. It uses some words that are identical or similar to those from standard English, but it also uses unique expressions and is spoken with a kind of singsong lilt. Here are some examples of Creole proverbs and translations obtained from the Web site Belizeans.com:

Creole: "Blood tika dan wata but wata tase betta."
Standard English: Blood is thicker than water, but water tastes better.

Creole: "U di deh di gren lik chesnat kat."
Standard English: You are there grinning like a cheshire cat.

Creole: "Ebre pat gat e kibber."
Standard English: Every pot has a cover.

Creole: "If dah no so, dah naily so."
Standard English: If it's not so, then it's nearly so.

characters in Belizean settings. Her first book was *Beka Lamb,* which was published in 1982. *Beka Lamb* is the story of a young Creole girl living in Belize City in the 1950s. Edgell followed this success with additional novels such as *In Times Like These* (1991) and *The Festival of San Joaquin* (1997). Other Belizean writers include Zoila Ellis, who has also won international acclaim, and local writers such as Evan Hyde, who writes about the black underclass, and David Ruiga, a Spanish writer.

There are now several magazines published in the country. The *Belize Review* is a general interest and ecotourism publication. *Belize Today* is a free magazine published by the government that contains information about current events, government activities, and other subjects. *Belize Network* is a monthly magazine about Belize available by subscription. Another publication is *Belizean Studies,* a scholarly research journal published three times a year by St. John's College.

In addition, Belize is home to a lively print media. The two oldest newspapers are highly political papers produced by the country's two political parties—the *Belize Times* (published by PUP) and the *Guardian* (published by UDP). Others include *Amandala* and the *Belize Reporter,* two more independent but very opinionated newspapers; the *Belize Government Gazette*, the country's official newspaper; and several local and tourist-oriented publications. *Amandala* is the largest independent paper. It is owned by Evan Hyde, founder of the United Black Association for Development (UBAD), Belize's version of the black power movement that was popular in the United States during the 1960s. The paper largely reflects Hyde's personal interests and views, which often focus on issues as diverse as basketball and homosexuality. Newspapers in Belize are rarely censored, but the quality of the country's journalism has been criticized by some.

VISUAL ARTS AND CRAFTS

The visual arts in Belize are probably less developed than its literature. Live theater is limited to productions put on by the Bliss Institute, a theater and arts center in Belize City that is the cultural heart of the city and the country. The center schedules regular art exhibits and performances by visiting theater and music groups. It also houses the National Library, which contains Mayan artifacts from the Caracol archaeological site. These events and exhibits tend to be pricey and are attended largely by the country's elite.

Film is also an underdeveloped medium in Belize. The country has only one movie theater, located in Belize City. In 2003 and 2004, however, Belize hosted an international film festival showcasing films from around the world. The festival created special categories for films made in Belize and by Caribbean filmmakers.

Other visual arts—such as paintings, sculptures, and craft items—have enjoyed a recent boom, due largely to the growth of the tourist industry. Painters, sculptors, and printers now display their works in a variety of exhibits and shops. Also, although Belize does not have the crafts tradition of some other Central American countries, local craftspeople produce items such as Mayan baskets and weavings, handmade pottery, and carvings made from mahogany and other local woods. A few Garifuna crafts may also be found, typically dolls or similar folk art. And the Mennonites make simple but beautiful wooden furniture.

MUSIC AND DANCE

Perhaps the most appealing and popular art forms in Belize are music and dance. Belizeans love music and dancing, but they prefer imported music styles popular in the Caribbean and Central America. For example, some of the most frequently heard pop music includes reggae from Jamaica, calypso from the Caribbean, and merengue from surrounding Latin countries. These types of music are played on numerous radio stations throughout Belize, and many of the country's musicians devote themselves to imitating these foreign musical styles.

Several forms of local music, however, have revived earlier Belizean musical traditions. The most notable is *punta* rock, a unique style of music based on traditional Garifuna song and drumbeat patterns. Numerous *punta* bands and performers play this music, including Andy Palacio, Bredda David, Chico Ramos, Titiman Flores, Sound Boys International, Griga Boyz, and the Punta Rebels. *Punta* rock is very popular in Belize and is gaining audiences in North America and Europe. The *punta,* a flirtatious and erotic dance done to *punta* rock music, is seen so often on the dance floors that it has become known as the unofficial national dance in Belize.

Yet another style of native Belizean music is a Creole calypso-like song pattern called breakdown (or *brukdown*), which features traditional African drums and other more unusual percussion devices. This music originated during the nineteenth century when groups of timber workers would travel from house to house and use any available household object, such as bottles, cans, or washbasins, to create an energetic type of music with spontaneous lyrics. Today, this music is making a comeback. One band in particular, Mr. Peters and his Boom and Chime Band, is developing an international reputation and has toured abroad.

CULTURAL FESTIVALS

Music and dance are a vital part of Belize's many cultural festivals and holidays. September is the height of these festivities, because two of the most significant events in the country's history are celebrated then. One is St. George's Cay Day (September 10), which commemorates a 1798 sea battle that helped end Spanish claims to Belize. The other is Inde-

A punta *rock group poses in Dangriga in southern Belize.* Punta *rock is based on traditional Garifuna music.*

pendence Day (September 21), the day in 1981 when British rule ended. During the September revelries, a party atmosphere prevails throughout the country. Shops are closed, restaurants do a booming business, and radios blare a mixture of patriotic and pop tunes. Belizeans everywhere watch parades, listen to speakers, and participate in official ceremonies. People also swarm by night to discos and by day to street fairs, which feature a bounty of food, live music, dancing, and fireworks.

The party continues on November 19, Garifuna Settlement Day, a holiday that celebrates the 1832 arrival of the Garifuna in Belize. The center of this celebration is in the southern Belize town of Dangriga, the home of the country's Garifuna community. The tradition for this day is a reenactment of the settlers' arrival in their small boats, or dories. As the reenactors arrive, they are greeted by revelers singing, beating drums, and waving Garifuna flags. Special dancers called John Canoe (or *Joncunu*) are also a traditional part of Garifuna Settlement Day. These dancers wear masks, flowing white tunics, feathered crowns, and hundreds of tiny shells attached to their knees. They travel from door to door dancing the *wanaragua*, a dance meant to imitate and mock the behavior of the white slave owners of past centuries.

Baron Bliss Day (March 9) is another popular holiday. It is a celebration of Henry Edward Ernest Victor Bliss IV, a wealthy Englishman who sailed to Belize in 1926. Bliss fell in love with the country and the kindness of Belizeans and decided to make it his home. Unfortunately, Bliss took ill from food poisoning and died aboard his ship before he could settle in Belize. He was so impressed by the country, however, that he left Belize close to $2 million in trust. This money has since been put to use to build health clinics, libraries, and other public improvements in Belize. The holiday is intended to honor Bliss for his contributions, and Belizeans celebrate the day with an annual yacht regatta, as well as horse and bicycle races throughout the country.

Other important events include national religious holidays and a number of local festivals. As in the United States, Christmas and Easter are dominated by family get-togethers, large meals, and church activities. One example of a local

Traditional drummers march in a parade celebrating Garifuna Settlement Day, a holiday marking the 1832 arrival of the Garifuna in Belize.

THE CREOLE BREAKDOWN

Part of the African/Creole tradition in the early days of the Belize colony was the breakdown, a type of music and dance that originated when the mahogany workers came home to Belize Town for a break to celebrate Christmas. Belizean folklorist Gladys Stuart, quoted in a Web site run by the Belize Arts Council, describes the scene at these celebrations, called *brukdowns* or *brams:*

> Groups of friends would gather at a home with the furniture pushed against the walls, leaving an open space in which to bram. Hips and bellies were gyrated, shoulders swing, and arms flung about with abandon, resulting in flowing contortions of the body while the legs kept up a rhythmic bram! bram! (If you were able to perform all the above then you could brukdown). Music was supplied by a combination of two or three of the following: drums, accordions, banjos, guitars, mouth organs, forks pulled across graters, pint bottles tapped against each other, combs covered with soft paper, brooms struck on the floor. Enthusiasm replaced harmony and the tempo increased as the liquor flowed—rum, rum popo, spruce and wines made from cashews, blackberries, oranges, craboos or ginger.

This music is still played in Belize by "boom and chime" bands that typically include a two-sided drum (which produces a bass sound, or boom, and a tenor sound, or chime), the jawbone of a donkey, a guitar, a banjo, and an accordion.

festival occurs in April, when the Maya celebrate the day of the patron saint, San Jose (or Saint Joseph). Other festivals include a coconut festival in May and a lobster festival in July hosted by the town of Cay Caulker. There is also a yearly cashew festival held in the town of Crooked Tree Village. Still other local events celebrate local arts and crafts. San Ignacio, for example, produces a yearly arts and crafts festival called the Cayo Expo, and in May there is a weeklong Toledo Festival of Arts showcasing schoolchildren's arts and crafts, such as baskets, paintings, and clay sculptures.

SPORTS AND LEISURE ACTIVITIES

In between the country's many festivals and celebrations, Belizeans entertain themselves with various sports and leisure activities. One of the most popular sports, soccer (called football in Belize), reflects the country's British heritage. National soccer competitions feature semiprofessional

Fishermen from Lamanai in central Belize display their day's catch. Fishing is a very popular pastime in Belize.

teams from each of the country's districts. Other popular sports, such as basketball and softball, are the result of American influences. In addition, cross-country cycling has become a big attraction, and there are many cycling competitions held around the country. Sports such as boxing, tennis, volleyball, and horse racing also have many fans and participants.

Other active Belizeans enjoy the many water sports available to them in their tropical paradise. Fishing is a traditional pastime and the way locals have fed their families for generations. Fish are abundant in Belize. As one resort Web site explains, "The estuaries, inlets and mouths to the many rivers are known for [fish species such as] . . . tarpon, snook and jacks. The lagoons and grass flats are known for the bonefish, permit and barracuda. The coral reefs support grouper, snapper, jacks and barracuda while the deeper waters off the drop off are home to sailfish, marlin, bonito and pompano."[19] Fish are caught from boats using bait and tackle or by underwater spearfishing. Today, however, fishing is closely regulated. For example, in order to prevent depleting fish populations, spearfishing is permitted only for divers who do not use scuba equipment. Other water activities popular among Belizeans include sailing and swimming.

In addition to sports and other outdoor activities, Belizeans enjoy everyday pleasures such as talking with neighbors and friends. Indeed, before radio and television were available in Belize, the main social activity was meeting at a local restaurant for drinks, gossip, and perhaps a game of checkers or dominoes. As scholar Irma McClaurin notes, "Everyone seems to know everyone else [in Belize], and gossip is perhaps third in popularity to football (soccer) and dominoes as a mass form of entertainment."[20] Similar socializing and gossip also often took place at church picnics or similar events. Today, Belizeans remain a social people, but much of the need for communication and social contact is met by radio talk shows and TV programs. Modern dance clubs and discos are also very popular meeting places for young Belizeans.

FOOD IN BELIZE

Belizeans also enjoy eating, although Belizean food cannot really be considered gourmet. One travel Web site, for example, describes the country's native cuisine as "a neglected art."[21] Nevertheless, the food in Belize reflects the variety of its cultures, especially its mix of Latin America and the Caribbean. Other influences include Mexican, Chinese, and American dishes. Indeed, visitors to Belize can find everything from Mexican empanadas to pizza, chow mein, and hamburgers.

Belize's national dish, however, consists of inexpensive rice and beans, reflecting the country's Creole roots as well as the continuing poverty within the society. Often, this dish is served with stewed chicken, pork, or beef, and accompanied by beer, soft drinks, or fresh-squeezed fruit juices such as lime, watermelon, and mango. Typical side dishes include coleslaw or fried plantains. Dessert is often homemade ice cream, a refreshing treat in Belize's hot climate. For breakfast, the staple food is the johnnycake (also called fry jack), a roll made of cornmeal that is fried to a golden crisp and served instead of toast.

Perhaps the country's most delicious local foods are the richly abundant fresh fish and shellfish. Seafood dishes such as lobster, shrimp, conch, snapper, or other fish fillets are offered almost everywhere in Belize. Other traditional fare includes cassava, a root that the Garifuna make into bread; tamales, a Latino specialty made from corn and meat boiled inside banana leaves; and *sere*, a Caribbean-style soup made with fish and coconut milk.

RADIO AND TELEVISION

The most popular forms of entertainment in Belize today are easily radio and television. For several decades, radio was the primary source of information in Belize. The first radio station, called Radio Belize, was created in 1952 in Belize City. It was funded by the colonial government and was originally modeled on the BBC, a British broadcasting station that is government funded but independent in content. Radio Belize quickly became a hit, and soon almost everyone in the country owned a radio. Radio became the focal point of people's lives. The station broadcasted everything from news to music to weather information. Before telephones were available in Belize, the station even aired personal messages, allowing people to communicate news about emergencies or the illnesses of relatives. The broadcasts, however, were in English, and much of the content was influenced by British tastes.

Radio Belize is still the country's main radio station, but today it is much more reflective of local culture. Its daily programming includes a variety of locally popular music, talk shows, and news, and it broadcasts in English, Spanish, and several other ethnic languages. As Internet writer Don Moore explains, "Radio Belize [sees] its role . . . [as] one of preserving Belizean culture against an onslaught of Americanisms."[22] Radio Belize also now has some competition, including an all-music station (Friends FM), a Spanish station (Estereo), and several local stations.

Radio's toughest competition, however, is television, which became available in Belize only in the 1980s. At first, television signals were pirated from Mexico and the United States, but now Belize has three television stations and cable is available in most cities and towns. Cable stations include familiar American entertainment and news channels such as HBO, STARZ!, Cinemax, Showtime, ABC, CBS, NBC, and FOX. For those in remote locations, satellite TV is available. Most Belizeans own their own TV set, and many spend

THE CASHEW FESTIVAL

One of the highlights for visitors to Belize is the Cashew Festival, a three-day celebration held annually during the first week of May in the village of Crooked Tree in northern Belize. Cashew trees are native to this area, and at the festival, people are invited to watch the harvest of the cashew. This is a multistep process in which the nut is separated from the fruit, toasted in its shell in a fire, and then shelled and roasted. Other delights during the festival include arts and crafts, an agricultural show, a display of village life, storytelling, a beauty pageant, and various Creole games. One such game is the greased pole climb. Perhaps the most popular festival treats, however, are the spicy Creole foods and sweet cashew wine, and the ever-present *punta* rock music, which inspires energetic dancing among festival participants.

a good deal of their time watching television. Some of the most popular programs are Mexican soap operas and American movies and sports events. This North American television exposure, however, has been criticized by some for promoting an American-style culture in Belize.

COMMUNICATION AND TRANSPORTATION

Citizens of Belize also have access to modern methods of communication. Many Belizeans have telephones, and Internet access became available in 1995. The latest reliable numbers from 1997, for example, show thirty-one thousand telephone lines and more than three thousand mobile phones in use. The phone system is rated above-average, with a network that depends primarily on microwave radio relay as well as one satellite station. In addition, two Internet providers offered service to about eighteen thousand Internet users as of 2002.

These methods of communication are especially important to people in Belize because communicating in person is often made difficult by the lack of easy transportation. Belize has only two main highways—the Northern Highway (running from the Mexican border into Belize City) and the Western Highway (which runs from Guatemala to Belize City)—and only these two and a few other highways are paved. In fact, as of 1998, more than 80 percent of all Belize's

This advertisement for an Internet bar in Belize City shows how popular the Internet has become in Belize in recent years.

roads were still gravel or dirt roads. And whether paved or not, all roads in Belize have deep potholes, which forces people to drive very slowly, often as slow as five to thirty miles per hour. Even today, the lack of good roads through the country's rugged terrain and numerous rain forests makes some parts of the country very difficult to reach.

In addition, many people cannot afford automobiles and there is no train system in Belize. Consequently, most people travel by bus. Although hardly luxurious, Belize's bus service is cheap and reliable, and buses run regularly between most cities and towns. Belize also has quite a few airports. One, located in Ladyville nine miles outside Belize City, is an international airport with flights to many foreign destinations as well as local flights to various cities in Belize. There are also numerous municipal airports, a few with paved runways. They offer flights between the country's cities on a regular basis.

Although still an undeveloped country by many measures, Belize nevertheless is embracing modern technology and learning to promote its rich cultural diversity alongside its natural resources.

6

Challenges Ahead

Belize has clearly outgrown its colonial roots and achieved a measure of political stability. Yet it now faces difficult new tasks. The nation is still struggling to grow its economy, provide for its people, and strengthen its political security. Moreover, perhaps Belize's biggest challenge for the future is to accomplish all these goals without sacrificing its true riches—its pristine environment, its diverse people and culture, and its relatively young democracy.

Economic Weaknesses

Experts say Belize's foremost challenge is to grow, stabilize, and diversify its economy. Although Belize has grown from its onetime single-crop economy (sugarcane) into trade of several products (sugar, bananas, citrus, shrimp, and lobster) and the new industry of ecotourism, this diversification has been only partly successful. Today, almost half of all Belizeans still earn their living in agriculture, and the country's economy remains largely dependent on just a few agricultural export products.

Also, despite another IMF-encouraged economic program that produced a trade surplus of $35 million in 1994, Belize still continues to import more goods than it exports. Profits earned from the country's exports provide only about two-thirds of what Belize pays to import needed goods such as food, fuel, machinery, and manufactured goods. As a result, the government has been spending more than it takes in, creating a growing foreign debt. To address these problems of overspending, the government was forced to freeze wages, reduce public services, and cut government jobs in the 1990s. These actions added to the already-existing problems of high unemployment and poverty.

Another part of the country's recent economic stimulation program involved privatization, the selling of government-owned businesses to private owners. Although this strategy was supposed to make the economy more efficient and productive, critics say it deprived the government of needed revenues and allowed foreign interests to gain control of critical Belize businesses. These concerns came to the forefront when two lucrative utilities—Belize Telecommunications Limited (BTL) and the Belize Electricity Company—were privatized. As researcher Minelva Brown-Johnson explains, "The decision of the government of Belize to relinquish controlling interest [in] the most viable and lucrative businesses in the country coupled with the fact that, based on the public sector deficit, it was not generating sufficient funds to cover its expenses, can be compared to shooting oneself in the foot."[23]

Meanwhile, Belize's ability to create new economic growth is hampered by certain inherent problems. For instance, although only about 15 percent of Belize's agricultural land is now being farmed, many of the large tracts of land suitable for development or agriculture are unreachable because of the country's poor road system. Economic experts say ex-

Nearly half of all Belizeans, like this Mayan farmer in San Miguel, earn a living in agriculture.

pensive infrastructure investments are therefore key to the economy's expansion. In addition, the tourism industry is limited by soaring land prices, a shortage of qualified labor (due to the emigration of many educated and qualified workers), and a lack of resources to build hotels, restaurants, and other facilities. Other problems slowing development include the high cost of commodities such as electricity and telephones.

Another weakness involves the degree of foreign ownership of Belizean industries. Much of the country's undeveloped agricultural land, for example, is still owned by foreign companies rather than by Belizeans. If these areas are developed, therefore, much of the profit will likely be taken out of Belize. Similarly, many of the investors in the newly developing tourism industry tend to be Americans or other foreigners. As a result, Belize benefits only from the creation of jobs and the sales of local goods to tourists, while larger profits go to the foreign owners.

FREE-TRADE THREATS

Furthermore, Belize's export economy remains vulnerable because it is dominated by trade relationships with only two countries—the United States and Britain. Most of Belize's products are sold to these two countries, largely because they have provided markets in which sales are guaranteed and are free of significant import taxes. Belize is a beneficiary of the Caribbean Basin Initiative (CBI), a U.S. government program designed to stimulate investment in Caribbean countries by offering tax-free access to the U.S. market for most Caribbean products. In addition, Belize is part of the Lomá Convention (replaced in 2000 by the Cotonou Agreement), a trade pact between the European Union (EU) and various African, Caribbean, and Pacific countries that provides preferential trade treatment in Europe for major agricultural products. Belize also has preferential trade relationships with neighboring countries under the Caribbean common market, CARICOM. These agreements have been crucial to Belize's successful marketing of its agricultural products, particularly its two most important crops—sugarcane and bananas.

These trade relationships, however, have come into question in recent years because of the global free trade movement. The United States and other developed nations have pushed for freer trade relationships in which all countries would trade on basically the same terms. As a result of this pressure, CARICOM began to move toward freer trade, a change that decreased the tariffs Belize could charge to non-Caribbean countries, thereby reducing Belize's income. The United States and various other countries have also challenged the EU preferential arrangements by lodging complaints with the World Trade Organization, a global organization that enforces free trade among participating nations. The WTO issued a ruling against the preferential treatment given by the EU to countries such as Belize. If such challenges succeed, they could seriously harm the Belize economy. Sugarcane and bananas, the country's two main crops, would be most affected. Since much of the country's workforce is employed in these agricultural industries, the result of a downturn would likely be even greater unemployment and poverty for the people of Belize.

LANDOWNERSHIP IN BELIZE

During much of Belize's history, large segments of its land have been owned by foreigners. Many of the foreign owners were large British companies originally involved in the mahogany trade. By the late nineteenth century, over 2.5 million acres of the country's best land belonged to only ninety-six owners, much of it owned by a single British company, the Belize Estate and Produce Company. As Belize's government became more empowered during the country's march toward independence, it took action to try to reduce the foreign ownership and control of Belizean land. In 1962, for example, the government passed a law giving tenant farmers more protection from eviction when companies wanted their land. In 1966 the government introduced the Land Tax Law, which imposed taxes on large land parcels, but most company landowners thwarted the law by lobbying for and gaining exemptions. Under the 1947 Land Acquisition Ordinance, the government began acquiring land from big landlords and redistributing it to the people. The government did this either by buying the land from foreign owners or by accepting title to the land in exchange for taxes owed to Belize. Between 1971 and 1982, approximately 525,000 acres were redistributed in this way to Belizean farmers. Finally, in 1973, the government passed the Alien Landholding Ordinance to limit the right of foreigners to buy and develop land in Belize. Despite these changes, most of Belize's best agricultural land continues to be owned by foreign interests. Much of this land, however, is still undeveloped and uncultivated because it lies in remote, inaccessible areas of Belize.

A group of Central American leaders, including Said Musa (fourth from right), attend a security and trade summit in Belize City in 2003.

Belize's government, under the leadership of PUP and Prime Minister Musa, has tried to address the weaknesses in the country's economy by lowering taxes to stimulate business investment and by borrowing money to finance public improvements and construction. Ambitious government projects, for example, have been initiated to build low-income housing and upgrade all major roads. Also, the government has targeted five economic sectors as potential growth areas: tourism, financial services, information technology, creative services, and research and development. These efforts have succeeded, at least in part. Economic growth indicators showed a dramatic increase between 1998 and 2000. The tourism industry in particular, thanks to government promotion, has recorded steady and significant growth. The number of tourists visiting the country has increased, and more than sixty hotels have been built since 1990. These range from world-class luxury establishments to family-run lodges and resorts.

The year 2001 brought a downturn in the economy, however. This was attributed primarily to two things: tropical storms and hurricanes that disrupted tourist activities and agriculture, and the reduced airline travel after the September 11 terrorist attacks in the United States. Also, because of increased government spending, the country's trade deficits and foreign debt have continued to grow.

Belize therefore still faces great economic challenges. Whether Belize can transform its economy from one dependent on agriculture and preferential trade toward new industries such as tourism, financial services, and other nontraditional industries—while at the same time maintaining control of government spending—remains an open question.

SOCIAL CONCERNS

Whether Belize can accomplish much-needed economic reforms and also protect its people and prevent a destabilization of its multicultural society is yet another challenge for Belize. Today, approximately one-third of Belizeans live in poverty, and this number is increasing as poor refugees from unstable surrounding countries flood into Belize's rural areas. In fact, Mestizos now make up close to 50 percent of Belize's poor. Many Maya also tend to be impoverished, and pockets of extreme poverty exist even in Belize City, the home of many Creole families. Most of the poor lack education and skills, and they are either unemployed or employed for low wages in agricultural jobs. These people have little hope of escaping their plight. They remain dependent on government programs for health care, food and housing assistance, and schooling for their children.

However, social programs to help the poor, already stretched to their limit, have been cut back in recent years as the government has tried to reduce its spending as part of economic reforms. Health and education were the most affected by government cuts. For example, expenditures for health care were reduced by $24 million per year in 1993 and 1994 and about $3 million per year during 1997 and 1998. Education was also affected, although increased international aid helped to offset these cuts. Other important social programs also were victims of the budget ax. These included the Rural Water Supply and Sanitation Program, the Conscious Youth Development Program, the School Feeding Program, and support for preschools. In addition to diminished resources, experts have pointed to a lack of planning and decision making among government ministries charged with helping the poor. Together, these problems result in the lack of an adequate safety net for the poor in Belize, a situation that could lead to even greater poverty.

Many believe that these problems of poverty are responsible for a rising level of crime and drug use in Belize. Crime and violence is said to have increased by 95 percent between 1991 and 1998, the same period that social programs were being cut. As Minelva Brown-Johnson explains, "Many [young people] are committing petty crimes or armed robberies and are peddling drugs to generate income for themselves to meet their basic needs."[24] In the larger urban areas, such as Belize City, the country has also witnessed an upsurge of youth gangs similar to those in urban areas of the United States. Other disturbing trends include rising domestic violence and prostitution.

The growing poverty, particularly among poor Mestizos, has the potential to create social and ethnic instability in Belize. Longer term residents, especially Creoles, have begun to feel threatened by Hispanics, whose presence is changing the ethnic makeup of Belize's society. Journalist and Belize

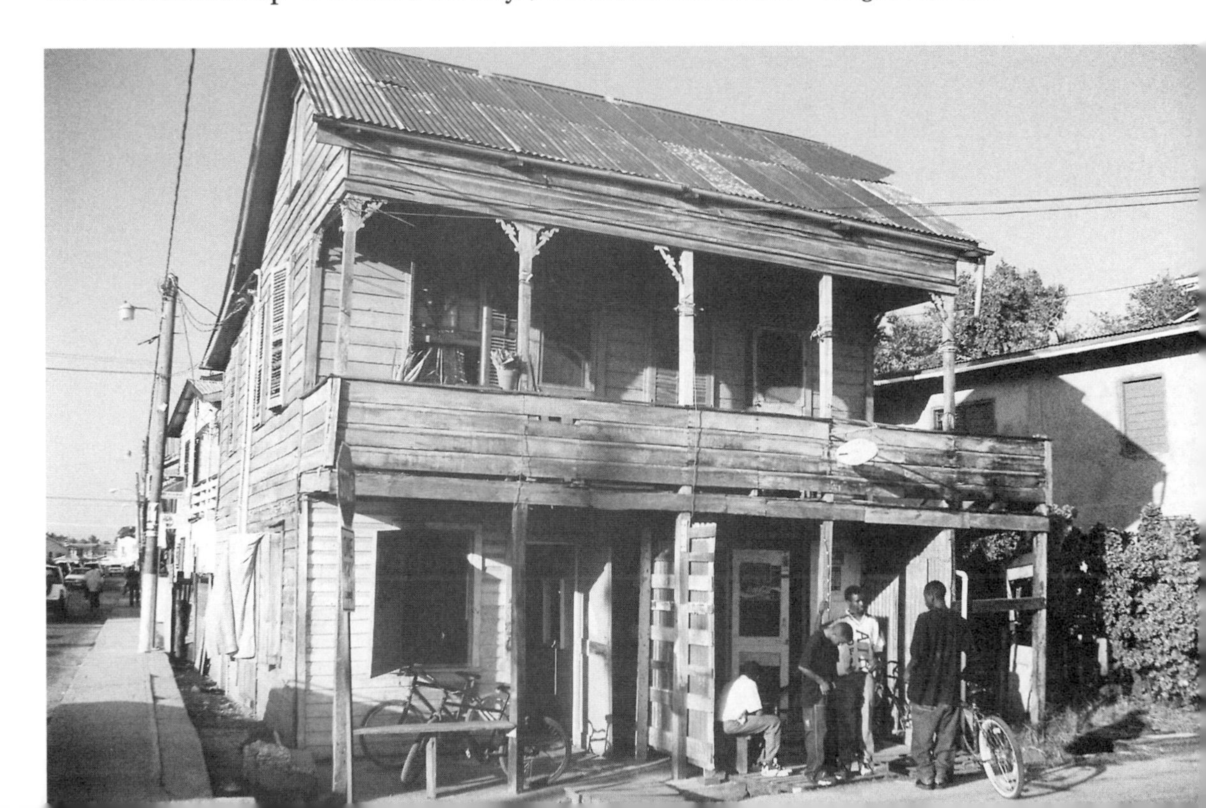

Several Belizean boys gather on the porch of a house in one of Belize City's poorer neighborhoods.

resident Meb Cutlack explains: "Belizeans share a desire to retain the established ethnic balance but there is a fear that it is fast being encroached upon by immigration into Belize from neighboring Spanish-speaking countries. . . . It is primarily a fear of losing that complex identity which calls itself Belize."[25] Rising ethnic tensions, if they continue, could disrupt Belize's historically peaceful social diversity. As Irma McClaurin explains, "Recent competition over jobs and other strategic resources has the potential to pit ethnic groups against one another in the future as the population struggles to survive in an atmosphere of shrinking natural resources and rising costs."[26] Like many other developing countries, therefore, Belize faces the difficult challenge of meeting the needs of a growing and impoverished population with limited economic resources.

ENVIRONMENTAL PRESERVATION

Yet another aspect of Belize's economic development is the importance of protecting its priceless environmental riches from development and tourist damage. Fortunately, Belizeans are becoming increasingly sensitive to this need to

THE DRUG TRADE IN BELIZE

In addition to poverty, crime, and high unemployment, Belize is plagued by a growing involvement in the South American drug trade. The country's long, unprotected coastline, its large, unpopulated interior, and the government's lack of resources to fight the illicit drug trade make the country an inviting site for drug traffickers wishing to move drugs into Mexico and the United States. As a result, in the 1990s the country became a small-scale producer of marijuana for the international drug trade as well as a major transshipment point for cocaine. In 1990, for example, Mexican police seized approximately 457 kilograms of cocaine that they believe had been smuggled into Mexico through Belize. The withdrawal of British forces in 1994 may have cleared the way for even greater drug activity in the country. In 1995 Belizean authorities in one raid seized more than half a ton (636 kilograms) of cocaine bound for the United States. As a result of this continuing drug activity, in 1996 the United States designated Belize a major drug transit country.

protect the environment. For example, a strong tourism organization, the Belize Tourism Industry Association (BTIA), has been created to promote the cautious development of ecotourism. The BTIA, together with environmental groups such as the Belize Audubon Society, favors sustainable development. This type of development places restrictions on development in order to protect environmentally sensitive areas.

Two tourists enjoy a boat tour through Crooked Tree Wildlife Sanctuary, one of many wildlife sanctuaries in Belize.

The Belizean government has already designated over 40 percent of the country as national parks, wildlife sanctuaries, and nature reserves. Two of these areas are the Crooked Tree Wildlife Sanctuary and the Cockscomb Basin Wildlife Sanctuary. The latter is the only jaguar reserve in the world. Other protected areas include nature reserves such as Bladen Branch, Burdon Canal, and Society Hall. In addition, the government has created sixteen large forest reserves and numerous national parks (Aguas Turbias, Blue Hole, Chiquibul, Five Blues Lake, Guanacaste Park, Laughing Bird Caye, Rio Blanco, Monkey Bay, Payne's Creek, and Sarstoon-Temash). Government protection is also given to marine life and ancient Mayan archaeological sites.

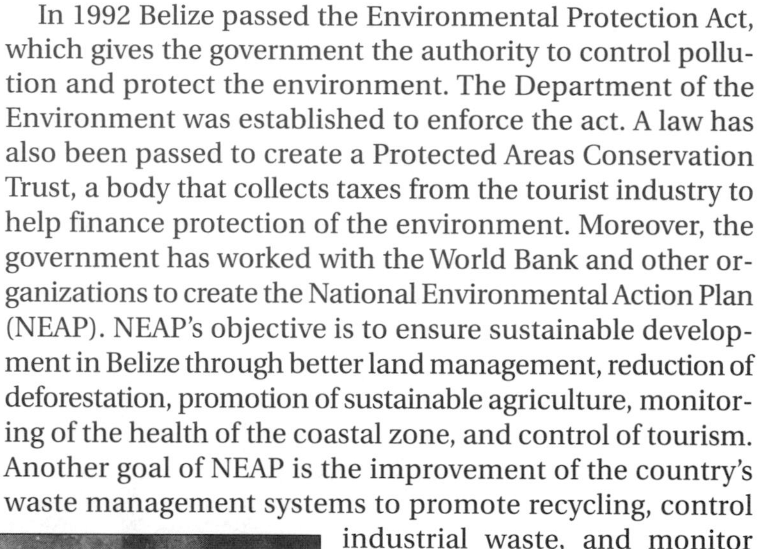

In 1992 Belize passed the Environmental Protection Act, which gives the government the authority to control pollution and protect the environment. The Department of the Environment was established to enforce the act. A law has also been passed to create a Protected Areas Conservation Trust, a body that collects taxes from the tourist industry to help finance protection of the environment. Moreover, the government has worked with the World Bank and other organizations to create the National Environmental Action Plan (NEAP). NEAP's objective is to ensure sustainable development in Belize through better land management, reduction of deforestation, promotion of sustainable agriculture, monitoring of the health of the coastal zone, and control of tourism. Another goal of NEAP is the improvement of the country's waste management systems to promote recycling, control industrial waste, and monitor water pollution. Belize is also a participant in various international agreements promising to protect endangered wildlife, promote biological diversity, and control pollution. These agreements include the Convention on International Trade in Endangered Species of Wild Fauna and Flora (CITES), the Convention on Biological Diversity, and the United Nations Framework Convention on Climate Change.

A sign in a protected nature reserve warns against hunting, planting crops ("milpas"), and logging.

Currently, however, environmental enforcement is weak, and no environmental cases have been prosecuted by the Belize government. In addition, critics charge that there are no regulations, guidelines, or other comprehensive plans for the development of Belize. They also claim that current laws permit government ministers to arbitrarily change the boundaries of any protected area to allow for development.

According to environmental writers Kimo Jolly and Ellen McRae, this allows "developers [to] target [ecotourist areas] for their own activities that could deprive the locals of both income and their environment's healthy future."[27]

The government will likely face increasing pressure to bend environmental protections as the population grows. In 2004, for example, to meet the country's needs for electricity, the government and the country's highest court approved the building of a hydroelectric dam in a rain forest area that is home to many endangered animal species. The country will probably face many more difficult decisions in the future regarding the caretaking of its environment. Given the rarity of its natural treasures and the importance of ecotourism to the Belize economy, both Belizeans and others around the world hope that the country will be motivated to protect its environmental riches from degradation.

POLITICAL REFORMS

Belize's success in reforming its economy, uplifting its people, and protecting its environment, in the end, will depend on the quality of its governance. Although the country has been praised repeatedly for its successful transition from a British colony to an independent democracy, many analysts today see problems in government that threaten the future of true democracy for Belize.

Critics say, for example, that under Belize's existing parliamentary system, the senate and even the democratically elected house tend to unconditionally approve decisions made by the cabinet ministers. This eliminates the separation of powers between the two branches of government and gives the executive branch virtually unchecked power. As political researcher and writer Dylan G. Vernon explains, "It results in a system where the very same persons both create legislation and policies, and execute them. Such a lack of [separation of powers] is seen by many as a central systemic constraint on accountability in governance in Belize."[28]

Furthermore, the cabinet ministers are already empowered under the constitution to amend laws without the legislative process and to grant exemptions from the paying of fees and taxes. This authority, combined with other weaknesses in the system, has turned the ministers into powerful politicians who control most of the country's public services and resources. It also has caused the people to bypass orderly bureaucratic processes and appeal directly to the ministers when they need something from the government. This practice has created an inefficient, unfair, and arbitrary political system, such as in the area of land distribution. Since the minister of lands has the final say on transfers of land, those who want access to land often contact the minister directly to improve their chances of success.

In addition, citizen participation in voting and government is low, with most people participating only by voting in elections once every five years. Recently, as a result of pressure from disgruntled citizens groups, a referendum system was created that allows citizens who collect a sufficient number of signatures to have their agendas included on voting ballots for changes that they seek to make in the country's laws.

Many people in Belize also complain of official corruption, particularly in the Public Service Ministry, which provides most government services in Belize. The ministry runs forty-four different departments and is the country's largest single employer. Public complaints have accused the ministry of poor service, lackadaisical attitudes, and high levels of financial corruption. Even public service employees themselves have made complaints, mostly about low pay. Other complaints suggest that there is little information available to the public about government purchases and borrowing and a lack of accountability in the awarding of public contracts. Some people think that government contracts are awarded on the basis of contributions businesses make to political campaigns. As Vernon notes, "There is a notable increase in the awarding of contracts just before a government leaves office, and shortly after the new one takes over. Allegations of kickbacks and bloated contracts are not uncommon."[29]

These and other problems have caused a large number of Belizeans to feel that their government is not responsive to their needs. A 1998 opinion poll, for example, found that an overwhelming 85 percent of Belize City residents thought the nation's democracy needed to be strengthened and that politicians were not to be trusted. A large majority of Belize City residents also felt that the justice system benefits the rich rather than the poor. The government's failure, under

RECOMMENDATIONS FOR POLITICAL REFORM

The Political Reform Commission, established to investigate problems with Belize's political system, issued its report in January 2000. The report, available at the government's Web site (www.belize.gov.bz), contained more than one hundred recommendations for change. The first two of these read:

> Recommendation 1: The Commission recommends that the system of national government in Belize continue to be based on the parliamentary executive model.
>
> Recommendation 2: The Commission recommends that the present political reform effort should focus attention on how to address the inadequacies of the current system and so improve the practice of Belizean democracy. In particular, the Commission urges that the following areas be urgently addressed by the Government and people of Belize:
>
> (a) Decreasing official waste and corruption;
>
> (b) Enhancing opportunities for people's participation in the legislative process;
>
> (c) Enhancing opportunities for women in political leadership;
>
> (d) Enacting campaign finance regulations;
>
> (e) Reviewing the role of the Senate in the legislative process;
>
> (f) Restoring faith in the independence of the Judiciary as the ultimate protector of constitutionally guaranteed rights and freedoms;
>
> (g) Enhancing the effectiveness and impartiality of the public service in the delivery of services to the Belizean public;
>
> (h) Ensuring greater oversight of the Legislature over the Executive branch of government;
>
> (i) Ensuring that elected officials and public officers who violate procedures and laws are held accountable;
>
> (j) Decreasing the divisiveness of partisan politics in the society;
>
> (k) Ensuring that Belizeans become more educated about their rights and about their political system;
>
> (l) Assessing if Belizeans want to retain a non-Belizean and monarchial Head of State.

both major political parties, to address the persistent and extreme poverty in the population has led to even more disillusionment among the country's poor population. In short, many Belizeans believe that the political system must be fundamentally reformed to create a truly stable and democratic nation.

To remedy some of these problems, the government passed several pieces of legislation in 1994. One law, the Ombudsman Act, created the Office of the Ombudsman to investigate complaints of wrongdoing by government ministries and employees. Belizeans seem to have welcomed the reform, and the ombudsman has already received many complaints, mostly about police brutality and land disputes. Other laws provide for the appointment of a contractor-general to oversee public contracts (Contractor-General Act); require elected officials (but not public employees) to annually disclose their assets (Prevention of Corruption in Public Life Act); and allow citizens to obtain government documents on request (Freedom of Information Act).

In addition, in response to a prolonged campaign by SPEAR, a well-known political advocacy group in Belize, the government established the Political Reform Commission in 1998 and charged it with reviewing the country's political system and developing proposals for reform. The commission completed its task in 2000 and made numerous recommendations. Foremost among them was a recommendation that the parliamentary system be retained but reformed to end corruption and promote greater democracy. Since then, the government has moved to implement some of the commission's recommendations. However, momentum has clearly slowed since the commission issued its report. Critics also complain that many of the anticorruption laws are routinely ignored by the government once they are passed.

With serious questions lingering about its economy, its increasing poverty, and its very democracy, Belize is clearly facing one of the most challenging times in its history. Its success or failure during the next few decades will determine its fate for many years to come.

Facts About Belize

Geography

Location: Central America; borders the Caribbean Sea, between Guatemala and Mexico

Area: 8,867 square miles (land: 8,805 square miles; water: 62 square miles)

Area comparative: Roughly the size of New Hampshire

Border countries: Guatemala and Mexico

Coastline: 239 miles

Climate: Tropical, very hot and humid; rainy season (May to November); dry season (February to May)

Terrain: Flat, swampy coastal plain; low mountains in the south

Natural resources: Timber, fish, hydropower, and arable land

Land use:

Arable land: 2.81%

Permanent crops: 1.1%

Other: 96.09% (1998 estimate)

Natural hazards: Frequent, devastating hurricanes (June to November) and coastal flooding (especially in the south)

Environmental issues: Deforestation; water pollution from sewage, industrial effluents, and agricultural runoff; solid and sewage waste disposal

People

Population: 272,945 (July 2004 estimate)

Age structure:
0–14 years: 40.6% (male, 56,530; female, 54,322)
15–64 years: 55.8% (male, 77,118; female, 75,309)
65 years and over: 3.5% (male, 4,674; female, 4,992)
(2004 estimate)

Birth rate: 28.89 births/1,000 population (2004 estimate)

Death rate: 6.04 deaths/1,000 population (2004 estimate)

Infant mortality rate: 26.37 deaths/1,000 live births (2004 estimate)

Life expectancy: Total population: 67.43 years (male, 65.11 years; female, 69.86 years) (2004 estimate)

Fertility rate: 3.77 children born/woman (2004 estimate)

Ethnic groups:
Mestizo: 48.7%
Creole: 24.9%
Maya: 10.6%
Garifuna: 6.1%
Other: 9.7%

Religions:

Roman Catholic: 49.6%

Protestant: 27% (Anglican, 5.3% Methodist, 3.5% Mennonites, 4.1% Seventh-Day Adventist, 5.2% Pentecostal, 7.4% Jehovah's Witnesses, 1.5%)

None: 9.4%

Other: 14% (2000 estimate)

Languages: English (official), Spanish, Mayan, Garifuna, Creole

Literacy rate for those age 15 and over: Total population: 94.1% (male, 94.1%; female, 94.1%)(2003 estimate)

GOVERNMENT

Country name: Belize (formerly British Honduras)

Government type: Parliamentary democracy

Capital: Belmopan

Administrative divisions: Six districts: Belize, Cayo, Corozal, Orange Walk, Stann Creek, and Toledo

National holiday: Independence Day, September 21

Date of independence: September 21, 1981 (from Great Britain)

Constitution: September 21, 1981

Legal system: Based on English law

Suffrage: 18 years of age; universal

Executive branch:

Chief of state: Queen Elizabeth II (since February 6, 1952), represented by Governor-General Sir Colville Young Sr. (since November 17, 1993)

Head of government: Prime Minister Said Wilbert Musa (since August 28, 1998)

Deputy Prime Minister: John Briceno (since September 1, 1998)

Cabinet: Appointed by the governor-general on the advice of the prime minister

Elections: The monarch is hereditary; the governor-general is appointed by the monarch; following legislative elections, the leader of the majority party or the leader of the majority coalition is usually appointed prime minister by the governor-general; the prime minister recommends the deputy prime minister.

Legislative branch:

Bicameral National Assembly: Consists of the senate (twelve members appointed by the governor-general—six on the advice of the prime minister, three on the advice of the leader of the opposition, and one each on the advice of the Belize Council of Churches and Evangelical Association of Churches, the Belize Chamber of Commerce and Industry and the Belize Better Business Bureau, and the National Trade Union Congress and the Civil Society Steering Committee) and the house of representatives (twenty-nine seats; members are elected by direct popular vote to serve five-year terms).

Judicial branch:

Supreme Court: The chief justice is appointed by the governor-general on the advice of the prime minister.

ECONOMY

Gross domestic product (GDP): $1.28 billion (2002 estimate)

Real growth: 3.7% (2002 estimate)

GDP per capita: $4,900 (2002 estimate)

GDP composition:

Agriculture: 18%

Industry: 24%

Services: 58% (2001 estimate)

Labor force: 90,000 (2001 estimate). (*Note:* There is a shortage of skilled labor and all types of technical personnel.)

Industries: Garment production, food processing, tourism, construction

Agriculture products: Bananas, cacao, citrus, sugar; fish, cultured shrimp; lumber

Exports: $207.8 million (2003 estimate)

Imports: $500.6 million (2003 estimate)

Debt: $475 million (2001 estimate)

Economic aid: $15 million (2000 estimate)

Currency: Belizean dollar (BZD)

NOTES

INTRODUCTION: AN UNTOUCHED JEWEL

1. Meb Cutlack, *Belize: Ecotourism in Action.* London: Macmillan Education, 2000, p. 14.

CHAPTER 1: A DIVERSE LAND

2. Ellen McRae, "Belize's Barrier Reef," in Huw Hennessey, ed., *Insight Guide: Guatemala, Belize, and the Yucatán.* Singapore: Apa, 2000, pp. 197–98.
3. Ben Greensfelder, Carolyn Miller, Conner Gorry, and Sandra Bao, *Belize, Guatemala, and Yucatán.* Victoria, Australia: Lonely Planet, 2001, p. 23.

CHAPTER 2: BELIZE'S COLONIAL PAST

4. Lynn V. Foster, *A Brief History of Central America.* New York: Facts On File, 2000, p. 24.
5. C.H. Grant, *The Making of Modern Belize.* Cambridge, England: Cambridge University Press, 1976, p. 41.
6. O. Nigel Bolland, *Belize: A New Nation in Central America.* Boulder, CO: Westview, 1986, p. 17.
7. Bolland, *Belize,* p. 36.

CHAPTER 3: NATIONHOOD FOR BELIZE

8. Ian Peedle, *Belize: A Guide to the People, Politics, and Culture.* New York: Interlink, 1999, p. 40.
9. Bolland, *Belize,* p. 110.
10. Bolland, *Belize,* p. 135.
11. Steven R. Harper, "Belize: Government and Politics," in Tim Merrill, ed., *Belize: A Country Study.* Washington,

DC: U.S. Government Printing Ofiice, 1993, p. 255.

12. Quoted in Julio A. Fernandez, *Belize: Case Study for Democracy in Central America.* Brookfield, VT: Gower, 1989, pp. 75–76.

CHAPTER 4: THE PEOPLE OF BELIZE

13. Peedle, *Belize,* p. 71.
14. Peedle, *Belize,* p. 72.
15. Charles C. Rutheiser, "Belize: The Society and Its Environment," in Tim Merrill, ed., *Guyana and Belize: Country Studies.* Washington, DC: U.S. Government Printing Office, 1993, p. 204.
16. Rutheiser, "Belize: The Society and Its Environment," p. 196.
17. Peedle, *Belize,* p. 64.

CHAPTER 5: CULTURE AND LIFESTYLE

18. Bolland, *Belize,* p. 62.
19. El Pescador Fishing Resort, "Fishing on Ambergris Caye." http://belizeone.com/pages/town/fishing.html.
20. Irma McClaurin, *Women of Belize: Gender and Change in Central America.* New Brunswick, NJ: Rutgers University Press, 1996, p. 26.
21. My Travel Guide, "Eating and Drinking in Belize." www.mytravelguide.com/city-guide/Central-America-&-Caribbean/Belize/Eating-and-drinking.
22. Don Moore, "Radio Belize: Caribbean Beat in Central America," 1989. www.swl.net/patepluma/central/misc/belize89.html.

CHAPTER 6: CHALLENGES AHEAD

23. Minelva Brown-Johnson, "Socio-Economic Analysis in the Context of Governance and Citizen Security," in Minelva Brown-Johnson, Dylan G. Vernon, and Shaun Finnetty, *Democratic Governance in Central America: The Case of Belize.* Managua, Nicaragua: Regional Coordination of

Economic and Social Research (CRIES), 2001, p. 35.

24. Brown-Johnson, "Socio-Economic Analysis in the Context of Governance and Citizen Security," p. 39.
25. Cutlack, *Belize*, p. 24.
26. McClaurin, *Women of Belize*, p. 29.
27. Kimo Jolly and Ellen McRae, *The Environment of Belize: Our Life Support System.* Benque Viejo del Carmen, Belize: Cubola Productions, 1998, p. 139.
28. Dylan G. Vernon, "Democratic Governance in Belize: Decay or Reform?" in Brown-Johnson et al., *Democratic Governance in Central America*, p. 52.
29. Vernon, "Democratic Governance in Belize: Decay or Reform?" p. 61.

Chronology

250–1000
A Mayan civilization develops and flourishes in northern Central America. (By 900–1000, the Maya reach Belize, Guatemala, western Honduras, and much of El Salvador.)

1502
Christopher Columbus travels to the Bay of Honduras and claims the surrounding area for Spain.

1508
Two Spanish explorers, Vicente Yáñez Pinzón and Juan Díaz de Solís, sail along the Caribbean coast of Belize into the Yucatán.

1655
Britain captures the territory of Jamaica and begins sending its buccaneers to establish settlements along the Caribbean coast. There, they raid Spanish ships carrying logwood.

1670
Britain signs the Treaty of Madrid, agreeing to suppress piracy, and British settlers begin harvesting their own logwood in the Belize area.

1763
The Seven Years' War between Spain and Britain ends with a treaty between the two countries (the Treaty of Paris) that gives Britain the right to harvest logwood in Belize but retains Spanish sovereignty over the territory. British Baymen establish more permanent settlements.

1787
Two thousand British settlers and their slaves arrive in Belize. They soon claim most of the land and create the first legislature (the Public Meeting).

1802
A small group of Garifuna settle in the area of Dangriga and become fishermen and farmers.

1820s
The Spanish empire in Central America disintegrates, and Guatemala claims that it has inherited Spain's sovereign rights over the Belize area.

1833
Britain abolishes slavery in all its colonies, including the Belize settlement.

1840s
A war in the Yucatán, the Guerra de las Castas, produces thousands of Mayan and Mestizo refugees, some of whom migrate into the Belize area.

1850s
When the dominant mahogany business in Belize declines, some big landowners start sugarcane farms.

1854
A formal constitution is established and an elected Legislative Assembly is created to replace the Public Meeting.

1859
Britain and Guatemala sign the Anglo-Guatemalan Treaty, which provides for the building of a road through Belize that links Guatemala with the Caribbean coast.

1862
The settlement of Belize is renamed British Honduras and officially declared a British colony.

1866–1872
A group of Maya led by Marcos Canul attack British settlements. Canul is killed by British troops in 1872.

1871
Britain increases its power over Belize by approving a new constitution, abolishing the Legislative Assembly, and appointing a new Legislative Council that is under British control.

1930s
The Great Depression shatters Belize's economy.

1931
A major hurricane hits Belize Town, the colony's main economic center.

1934
Poor people begin to protest the country's dismal economic conditions. A broad protest movement, led by Antonio Soberanis Gómez and called the Labourers and Unemployed Association (LUA), is formed.

1939
Six Creoles who are more sympathetic toward labor are elected to the Belize Town Board.

1940s
Trade unions are legalized, creating the General Workers' Union (GWU). The LUA and the GWU together criticize the colonial political system.

1945
The Guatemalan government declares Belize part of Guatemala.

1949
The British governor of British Honduras devalues the colony's currency, leading to the formation of a People's Committee to oppose colonial rule.

1950
The People's Committee is replaced by the People's United Party (PUP), which successfully pushes for government and election reforms.

1954
A new constitution is adopted providing for universal suffrage and an elected legislature. PUP candidates win eight of the nine elected seats in the new Legislative Assembly.

1960
A constitutional conference is held in London, leading to greater self-government for the colony.

1963
Guatemala breaks off negotiations with Britain and threatens war against Belize.

1964
The colonial government in Belize is given control over most internal matters. Britain, however, maintains control over internal security, foreign policy, and defense.

1973
The colony's name is officially changed to Belize. The United Democratic Party (UDP) is formed to oppose PUP.

1975
Britain allows the colonial government to participate in international diplomacy.

1976
Frustrated by their inability to resolve the dispute with Guatemala, Britain and Belize seek international support for Belizean independence.

1979
Refugees from civil wars in El Salvador and Guatemala begin flowing into Belize.

1980
The United Nations passes a resolution demanding independence for Belize no later than the end of 1981.

1981
Belize becomes independent on September 21 and George Price, leader of PUP, becomes the first prime minister.

1984
UDP wins the elections and UDP leader Manuel Esquivel becomes Belize's second prime minister. Sugar prices drop, creating an economic crisis. Belize gets a loan from the International Monetary Fund and implements an economic program.

1989
PUP wins elections in Belize.

1990
Tourism begins to earn substantial revenues.

1991
Guatemala recognizes Belize as an independent country and the two countries establish diplomatic relations, but their dispute remains unresolved.

1992
Belize passes the Environmental Protection Act.

1993
UDP wins elections in Belize.

1994
Britain withdraws all permanent troops from Belize.

1995
Belize passes several anticorruption and freedom of information laws.

1998
PUP wins elections in a landslide, promising political reforms; PUP leader Said Musa becomes Belize's third prime minister. The government establishes a Political Reform Commission.

2000
The Political Reform Commission releases its report calling for major political reforms.

2001
Hurricanes and the September 11 terrorist attacks in the United States create an economic downturn in Belize.

2003
Musa wins a second term as prime minister.

For Further Reading

Books

Diane Kelsay Harvey, *Fishing with Peter.* Wilsonville, OR: Beautiful America, 1993. A young-adult book discussing brown pelicans and other fishing birds of Belize's coastal waters.

Leslie Jermyn, *Cultures of the World: Belize.* New York: Marshall Cavendish, 2001. An overview of Belize, including geography, history, government, economy, lifestyle, religion, and many other topics.

Richard Mahler, *Belize: Adventures in Nature.* Santa Fe, NM: J. Muir, 1997. A guidebook focusing on Belize's natural resources. It also includes information about travel, climate, cuisine, flora and fauna, and many other topics.

Caitlin Maynard, *Rainforests and Reefs: A Kid's-Eye View of the Tropics.* New York: Franklin Watts, 1996. An account of a trip to Belize by the Junior Zoologists Club of the Cincinnati Zoo and Botanical Garden. The description of the journey provides an entertaining view of Belize's diversity of plants and animals.

Marion Morrison, *Enchantment of the World: Belize.* New York: Childrens Press, 1996. Describes the history, geography, culture, people, and economy of Belize for young-adult readers.

Web Sites

Belize Consular Information Sheet (http://travel.state.gov/travel/belize.html). A U.S. government Web site providing practical information and travel warnings for people who plan to visit Belize.

A History of Belize, Nation in the Making (www.belizenet.com/history/toc.html). An Internet adaptation of a book on the history of Belize. Produced by a Belizean publishing company, Cubola Productions, this site provides an understandable and detailed history of the country.

Travel Belize (www.travelbelize.org). The official Web site of the Belize Tourist Board provides background on the country's history, culture, geography, and government, as well as information about tourist attractions and getting around in Belize.

The World Factbook: Belize (www.cia.gov/cia/publications/factbook/geos/bh.html). This U.S. government site gives geographical, political, economic, and other information on Belize.

WORKS CONSULTED

BOOKS

O. Nigel Bolland, *Belize: A New Nation in Central America.* Boulder, CO: Westview, 1986. A profile of Belize that covers history, culture, economy, politics, and foreign relations.

Minelva Brown-Johnson, Dylan G. Vernon, and Shaun Finnetty, *Democratic Governance in Central America: The Case of Belize.* Managua, Nicaragua: Regional Coordination of Economic and Social Research (CRIES), 2001. A scholarly presentation of the economic, political, and criminal aspects of Belizean society prepared by regional research and democratic advocacy groups.

Meb Cutlack, *Belize: Ecotourism in Action.* London: Macmillan Education, 2000. A guide to Belize, its environment, people, culture, and customs, both past and present.

Julio A. Fernandez, *Belize: Case Study for Democracy in Central America.* Brookfield, VT: Gower, 1989. A study of Belize's political system by a political scientist who is a native of the country.

Lynn V. Foster, *A Brief History of Central America.* New York: Facts On File, 2000. A comprehensive history of Central America, beginning with early cultures and concluding with analyses of the political and economic challenges facing countries of the region.

C.H. Grant, *The Making of Modern Belize.* Cambridge, England: Cambridge University Press, 1976. A scholarly discussion of Belize's development from colonialism toward independence.

Ben Greensfelder, Carolyn Miller, Conner Gorry, and Sandra Bao, *Belize, Guatemala, and Yucatán.* Victoria, Australia: Lonely Planet, 2001. A tourist guidebook on Belize, Guatemala, and surrounding areas by a popular publisher of travel materials.

Hum Hennessy, *Insight Guide: Guatemala, Belize, and the Yucatán.* Singapore: Apa, 2000. A travel guide to Belize, Guatelmala, and the Yucatán from a leading travel publisher; contains useful information on the Maya, flora and fauna, and Belize's barrier reef.

Kimo Jolly and Ellen McRae, *The Environment of Belize: Our Life Support System.* Benque Viejo del Carmen, Belize: Cubola Productions, 1998. A student guide to Belize's unique ecosystems and environmental policies from a Belize-based publishing company.

Vivien Lougheed, *Adventure Guide to Belize.* Edison, NJ: Hunter, 2003. A comprehensive travel guidebook containing background on Belize's history, culture, government, economy, climate, flora, and fauna, as well as practical travel information.

Irma McClaurin, *Women of Belize: Gender and Change in Central America.* New Brunswick, NJ: Rutgers University Press, 1996. A scholarly study of the women of Belize and the effort to change the gender roles, ideas, and attitudes that limit their lifestyle and opportunities.

Tim Merrill, ed., *Belize: A Country Study.* Washington, DC: U.S. Government Printing Office, 1993. A Library of Congress report on Belize that provides a good overview of its history, society, economy, government, military, and foreign policy.

Ian Peedle, *Belize: A Guide to the People, Politics, and Culture.* New York: Interlink, 1999. An authoritative and readable guide to the history, environment, culture, and economy of Belize.

———, *A Geography of Belize: The Land and Its People.* Benque Viejo del Carmen, Belize: Cubola Productions, 1997. An exploration of Belize's land and its people by a Belize-based publishing company.

Periodicals

Meb Cutlack, "When the Dollars Run Out: Belize Keeps Selling Off Its Assets to Foreign Companies. Now the Country Is Bleeding Itself Dry to Pay Electricity, Telephone and Water Bills," *New Statesman,* March 4, 2002.

Colin Woodard, "Border Brawl," *Bulletin of the Atomic Scientists,* November 2000.

———, "Wildlife Loses Out in Ruling on Belize Dam," *New Scientist,* February 7, 2004.

INTERNET SOURCES

Barbara Bates-Wurst, "Garifuna." www.mnsu.edu/emuseum/ cultural/mesoamerica/garifuna.html.

"Belize—Culture Overview." http://expedition.bensenville.lib.il.us/CentralAmerica/Belize/culture.htm.

Belize Arts Council, "The Creole." www.belizemall.com/bac/creole.html.

Belize Audubon Society, "Cockscomb Basin Wildlife Sanctuary." www.belizeaudubon.org/html/parks/cbws.htm.

Belize.com, "60 Seconds to NAFTA." www.belize.com/invest.html.

Belize Social Security Board, "Benefits in Brief," 2001–2003. www.socialsecurity.org.bz/beneficiaries/brief.html.

Belize Trade and Investment Development Service (Beltraide), *Trade and Investment Monitor,* February 17, 2004. www.belizeinvest.org.bz/index.php.

Belizeans.com, "Grauma use to seh . . . ," June 3, 2002. www.belizeans.com/grauma.htm.

Cornerstone Foundation, "The Arts in Belize, Central America." www.peacecorner.org/art_and_music.htm.

El Pescador Fishing Resort, "Fishing on Ambergris Caye." http://belizeone.com/pages/town/fishing.html.

FreeDictionary.com, "Economy of Belize." http://encyclopedia.thefreedictionary.com/Economy%;20of%;20Belize.

Government of Belize, "About Belize." www.belize.gov.bz/belize/welcome.shtml.

———, "Final Report of the Political Reform Commission," January 2000. www.belize.gov.bz/library/political_re form/welcome.html.

———, "Profile of Prime Minister Said W. Musa." www.belize.gov.bz/pm/bio.html.

"Letter from the President to the Chairmen and Ranking Members of the Senate Committee on Foreign Relations, the Senate Committee on Appropriations, the House Committee on Appropriations, and the House Committee on International Relations," February 22, 1996. www.lectlaw.com/files/drg22.htm.

Don Moore, "Radio Belize: Caribbean Beat in Central America," 1989. www.swl.net/patepluma/central/misc/belize89.html.

My Travel Guide, "Belize Tourism." www.mytravelguide.com/city-guide/Central-America-&-Caribbean/Belize/Belize.

———, "Eating and Drinking in Belize." www.mytravelguide.com/city-guide/Central-America-&-Caribbean/Belize/ Eating-and-drinking.

National Geographic, "Blue Hole, Lighthouse Reef, Belize," 2002. www.nationalgeographic.com/photography/ galleries/belize/photo2.html.

Angel Nuñez, "'El Duende'—San Pedro Folklore." www.ambergriscaye.com/25years/elduende.html

———, "'El Sisimito'—San Pedro Folklore." www.ambergriscaye.com/25years/elsisimito.html.

———, "'La X'tabai'—San Pedro Folklore." www.ambergriscaye.com/25years/laxtabai.html.

Herbert Panton, "The Anti-Corruption and Transparency Roads Are Already Paved with Legislation," 2004. www.spear.org.bz/story3.html.

Jacqueline Dow Pratt, "History of Agriculture in Belize," 2004. www.personal.psu.edu/users/j/d/jdp945/belize/historyofag.htm.

Thinkquest, "Western Rainforest of Belize." http://library.thinkquest.org/27507/belize.htm?tqskip1=1.

U.S. Department of State, Bureau of Democracy, Human Rights, and Labor, "Belize: Country Reports on Human Rights Practices—2003," Feburary 25, 2004. http://us.

politinfo.com/Information/Human_Rights/country_report_2003_135.html.

U.S. Department of State, "FY 2001 Country Commercial Guide: Belize." www.state.gov/www/about_state/business/com_guides/2001/wha/belize_ccg2001.pdf.

U.S. Embassy Belize, "Country Commercial Guide—Belize," 2002. http://usembassy.state.gov/belize/wwwhcountry commercialguide.html.

World Trade Organization, "Trade Policy Review: Belize: WTO Commitments Could Anchor Future Reform Efforts Needed to Sustain Growth," July 14, 2004. www.wto.org/english/tra top_e/tpr_e/tp233_e.htm.

INDEX

Picture Credits

Cover: John Elk III/Lonely Planet Images
AP/Wide World Photos, 18, 45, 79
© Bettmann/CORBIS, 23, 26, 36, 41
Tom Boyden/Lonely Planet Images, 15
© Macduff Everton/CORBIS, 49, 70, 76
Lee Foster/Lonely Planet Images, 46
© Jeff Greenberg/The Image Works, 59
Robert Harding/World Imagery, 68
Hulton Archive/Getty Images, 29
© Hulton-Deutsch Collection/CORBIS, 38
Greg Johnston/Lonely Planet Images, 14
© Steve Kaufman/CORBIS, 83
Daniel LeClair/Reuters/Landov, 43
© Alain Le Garsmeur/CORBIS, 52
Andrew Marshall and Leanne Walker/Lonely Planet Images, 25
Doug McKinley/Lonely Planet Images, 74
© Keri Pickett/WorldPictureNews, 51
Reuters/Landov, 30
© David Samuel Robbins/CORBIS, 63
© Joel W. Rogers/CORBIS, 54
© Kevin Schafer/CORBIS, 10, 20, 47, 60, 84
© James Sparshatt/CORBIS, 81
Stone, 67
Mark Webster/Lonely Planet Images, 5, 13
Steve Zmina, 6, 9

About the Author

Debra A. Miller is a writer and lawyer with a passion for current events and history. She began her law career in Washington, D.C., where she worked on legislative, policy, and legal matters in government, public interest, and private law firm positions. She now lives with her husband in Encinitas, California. She has written and edited publications for legal publishers as well as numerous books and anthologies on historical and political topics.